SWAMI VIVEKANANDA

TORCHBEARER OF THE MASTER-DISCIPLE RELATIONSHIP

Also by Sirshree

Spiritual Masterpieces – Self Realisation books for serious seekers

Who Am I Now: From mindfulness to no-mind
The Secret of Awakening
100% Karma: Learn the Art of Conscious Karma that Liberates
100% Wisdom: Wisdom that leads you to experience and be established in your true nature
100% Meditation: Dip into the Stillness of Pure Awareness
You are Meditation: Discover Peace and Bliss Within
Essence of Devotion: From Devotee to Divinity
The Unshaken Mind: Discovering the Purpose, Power and Potential of your mind
The Supreme Quest: Your search for the Truth ends there where you are
The Greatest Freedom: Discover the key to an Awakened Living
Secret of The Third Side of The Coin: Unravelling Missing Links in Spirituality
Seek Forgiveness & be Free: Liberation from Karmic Bondage
Passwords to a Happy Life: The Art of Being Happy in all Situations

Self Help Treasures – Self Development books for success seekers

The Source of Health: The Key to Perfect Health Discovery
Inner Ninety Hidden Infinity: How to build your book of values
Inner 90 for Youth: The secret of reaching and staying at the peak of success
The Source for Youth: You have the power to change your life
Inner Magic: The Power of self-talk
Self Encounter: The Complete Path - Self Development to Self Realization
The Five Supreme Secrets of Life: Unveiling the Ways to Attain Wealth, Love and God
You are Not Lazy: A story of shifting from Laziness to Success
Freedom From Fear, Worry, Anger: How to be cool, calm and courageous
The Little Gita of Problem Solving: Gift of 18 Solutions to Any Problem
Freedom From Failure: 7 Spiritual Secrets That Transform Failure Into A Blessing

New Age Nuggets – Practical books on applied spirituality and self help

The Source: Power of Happy Thoughts
Secret of Happiness: Instant Happiness - Here and Now!
Excuse me God...: Fulfilling your wishes through the Power of Prayer and Seed of Faith
Help God to Help You: Whatever you do, do it with a smile
Ultimate Purpose of Success: Achieving Success in all five aspects of life
Celebrating Relationships: Bringing Love, Life, Laughter in Your Relations
Everything is a Game of Beliefs: Understanding is the Whole Thing
Detachment From Attachment: Gift of Freedom From Suffering
Emotional Freedom Through Spiritual Wisdom: How to Take Charge of Your Emotions

Profound Parables – Fiction books containing profound truths

Beyond Life: Conversations on Life After Death
The One Above: What if God was your neighbour?
The Warrior's Mirror: The Path To Peace
Master of Siddhartha: Revealing the Truth of Life and After-life
Put Stress to Rest: Utilizing Stress to Make Progress
The Source @ Work: A Story of Inspiration from Jeeodee

SWAMI VIVEKANANDA

TORCHBEARER OF THE MASTER-DISCIPLE RELATIONSHIP

Sirshree

PRABHAT PRAKASHAN

ISO 9001: 2015 Publishers

Published by
PRABHAT PRAKASHAN
4/19 Asaf Ali Road,
New Delhi-110 002 (INDIA)
Tele : +91-11-23289777
e-mail: prabhatbooks@gmail.com

ISBN 978-93-5266-598-3
SWAMI VIVEKANANDA
TORCHBEARER OF THE MASTER-DISCIPLE RELATIONSHIP
by Sirshree Tejparkhi

Edition
First, 2019

Price
₹ 300.00 (Rupees Three Hundred only)

Printed at
R-Tech Offset Printers, Delhi

To those disciples, who gave more importance to following the teachings of their guru than their intellect and dedicated themselves to the service of humanity.

Contents

PART – 3
Expression of Discernment and Devotion

Introduction
Two Elements One Essence

There has been an unmatched master-disciple pair in India that is illustrated world over today. This pair is that of Ramakrishna Paramhansa and Swami Vivekananda.

If Swami Vivekananda is the crown of the temple of Indian spirituality, his master Ramakrishna Paramhansa is its foundation stone. The stone that is not visible otherwise, but without which, the idea of the main building cannot be conceived. Therefore, whenever Swami Vivekananda is remembered, memories of Ramakrishna Paramhansa naturally come alive. Their relationship is an epitome of the master-disciple tradition. Ramakrishna Paramhansa is an inseparable part of Swami Vivekananda's life. Swami Vivekananda's quest for Truth culminated at the feet of Ramakrishna Paramhansa, and after that, he propagated the teachings of his master to the wide world.

Though Narendra was a son of Vishwanath Dutt, he was also considered as the essence of Lord Rama and Lord Krishna. He found his guru in the form of Ramakrishna Paramhansa. The story that unfolded after that demonstrates the qualities that a seeker of Truth should imbibe. Ramakrishna Paramhansa was an extraordinary guru, and Swami Vivekananda was an exemplary disciple. While the master revelled in the bliss of the heart, the disciple delighted in intellectual heights. It was a unique combination that makes this pair exceptional.

If Swami Vivekananda was not convinced upon anything, he used to argue with Ramakrishna Paramhansa until he was convinced. It was as if that's the way he wanted to grasp his guru's teachings. It was so because he was an intellectual.

Swami Vivekananda, who was known as Narendra Dutt in his childhood, was courageous and inquisitive by nature. When his mother was pregnant, she used to have divine dreams. In one such dream, she saw Lord Shiva coming and sitting quietly in her lap. It was as if this dream was heralding the future of her illustrious son.

Narendra, who was wandering in search of the supreme Truth and God, attained both after meeting Ramakrishna Paramhansa and thus he became his devout disciple. However, Narendra did not readily accept Ramakrishna Paramhansa as his guru. He not only assessed Ramakrishna Paramhansa logically but also worked upon himself to become a deserving disciple. As a result, he could receive all those spiritual treasures from his master, which other disciples remained deprived of.

This great Indian monk, as he was popularly known for his early visits outside India, made the whole world his field of karma. With the inspiration of his master, he promoted and propagated the Indian culture, civility and religion all around. He influenced many intellectuals with his remarkable wisdom and talent.

We can learn about the strength of Swami Vivekananda's character from some instances of his life. He maintained the purity of his character in some of the most adverse circumstances. He continued to shine like the Sun and spread the light of his wisdom wherever he went.

After the death of Ramakrishna Paramhansa, he established the "Ramakrishna Math" and the "Ramakrishna Mission" in the memory of his master. Many schools, hospitals and social organisations being run by the Mission continue to serve humanity.

After attaining knowledge from Ramakrishna Paramhansa, Swami Vivekananda established himself as a great personality. He immensely inspired the youth by his message, "Be great and help others become great." His life, works and message continue to inspire one and all even today. He taught the youth to walk on the path of Truth and serve society selflessly without expecting anything in return. His birthday on 12th January is celebrated as "National Youth Day" to commemorate his service for the youth.

Swami Vivekananda noticed several shortcomings in the youth of his time, and he guided them accordingly. Primarily, these shortcomings were the lack of courage and fearlessness. He also noticed despondency amongst the youth.

He invigorated the youth with his stirring words: "My countrymen should have nerves of steel, muscles of iron and minds like a thunderbolt!"

He emphasised strength and said, "If there is a sin, this is the only sin to say that you are weak, or others are weak." While saying so, he encouraged the youth to inculcate four types of strength within themselves – strength of character, physical strength, mental strength and spiritual strength. He believed that the one who has attained these strengths alone could conquer his mind. True to this belief, he was the absolute master of his mind. The term "Swami" aptly suits his personality.

Lethargy is a curse for today's youth. Therefore, young people must read such life-stories to know how great personalities have toiled their way, how they have overcome their lethargy as well as hyperactivity. The youth can gain such inspiration by reading the biography of Swami Vivekananda.

Swami Vivekananda passed away at a very young age of 39 years. However, in such a short lifespan, with the inspiration of Ramakrishna Paramhansa, the light of wisdom he spread the world over would always be remembered.

The master and disciple duo of Swami Vivekananda and Ramakrishna Paramhansa were so closely connected that they seemed incomplete without each other. Those who read about renowned spiritual personalities would know that often the names of their masters or disciples are not easily remembered. Very few may remember the name of the best disciple of Lord Mahavira or the names of the disciples of Guru Nanak and Saint Kabir. Similarly, one may have to think hard to recall the names of the masters of Saint Kabir or Saint Mira. It is so because they did not become famous. Saint Kabir's guru, Ramanand, and Saint Mira's guru, Saint Ravidas, would not come to one's mind instantly. But Saint Mira and Saint Kabir are world famous. Likewise, Guru Angad, the disciple of Guru Nanak, is known to very few people. In some cases, the disciples became famous and in some other cases the masters. This is not so in the case of Swami Vivekananda and Ramakrishna Paramhansa. The name of one naturally brings to mind the name of the other.

The life of Swami Vivekananda shows the brilliant expression that can be manifested in such a short life when both the heart and the intellect work together in tandem.

Besides a few inspiring incidents from the lives of Swami Vivekananda and Ramakrishna Paramhansa, this book also narrates their ideas and mutual affection for each other. On reading this book, you will come to know how a master grooms his disciple through teaching, training, and testing. This book will provide you with an opportunity to witness how a master and his disciple can symbolise the term "two bodies and one soul." Hope reading this book helps you revel in the bliss of higher understanding.

PART – 1

The Journey of a Seeker of Truth

1
Beginning of the Journey

Arise, awake and stop not till the goal is reached.

O Lord of the body, mind, and intellect!

When something gets associated with the body, the body becomes instrumental in serving the purpose of the lord.

When something gets associated with the mind, the mind becomes steadfast, obedient, unshaken and loving.

When something gets associated with the intellect, the power of discernment awakens within.

With the awakened body, mind and intellect awaken the bliss of wisdom – Vivekananda!

What is this "something" that needs to be associated with everything to derive the bliss of wisdom? You are going to discover this "something" in this book. Find it in this book and connect with your true self to awaken the Vivekananda within you.

When did this "something" get associated with Swami Vivekananda? Let us get a glimpse of it.

It was midnight. As Narendra saw dark clouds in the sky, he could see the darkness spread over his mind, and he could hardly see any ray of hope. Clouds thundered, and lightning struck. Lost in his thoughts, Narendra was walking barefoot towards his house. His feet were not supporting his body. It was as if they were pleading him to rest for a while. But, he was numb to his body as his mind was elsewhere.

Suddenly, there was a heavy downpour, and in less than a moment, Narendra was completely drenched. Defeated, he sat in the middle of the empty road and pleaded with folded hands, "O Lord, what are you punishing me for? There are so many sinful people in this world, but sparing them all, why are you punishing me? Is it because I have faith in you? Is this your way to justice?"

Narendra's eyes were filled with tears of sorrow. Suddenly, he heard a voice within. His conscience asked him, "One who wants pleasure does not consider the method of acquiring it. First, decide what you want – position, fame, wealth, comforts?"

His logical mind replied, "I want wealth, but through the path of righteousness."

His conscience alerted him, "You will attain God on the path of righteousness, not wealth! What do you want – God, or wealth and comforts?"

Narendra screamed, "God, God, and God alone!"

His conscience replied, "Then don't ask for comforts and conveniences. You can never attain God if you get entangled in worldly pleasures. God can be attained by conquering your mind through the process of austerity and penance."

This ended the dilemma that was going on inside Narendra. He listened to his conscience. The negative thoughts that were clouding his mind vanished, dispelling the darkness of his life. Meanwhile, the clouds in the sky had also dispersed, revealing a divine resplendent aura, as it were. All the doubts were being put to rest and the turmoil in his mind was beginning to settle down. "Something" had got associated with his intellect that awakened the power of discretion within him and directed him to his guru, and thus he became Swami Vivekananda. The first ray of light on that day dissolved not only the darkness prevailing outside but also the darkness in Narendra's mind. His intellect was radiant with the new light. Now, he knew what he wanted to do.

This is the story of Vivekananda, whose wisdom had awakened. It is only when the wisdom awakens, does one start his journey on the path of Truth. Therefore, the story of Vivekananda ought to be seen as the story of every earnest Truth seeker.

Vivekananda, formerly known as Narendra Dutt, was born on 12th January 1863; however, the devotee, Narendra was born twenty-five years later. It was as if he was reborn into divine devotion. First was the birth of his body, while the other was the culmination of limiting personalised beliefs and awakening of the true Self in his body, which is also called Self-realization, the experience of *Sat-Chit-Ananda.*

After reading this book, you will understand what happened during this journey to bliss, what was born and what happened around. Understanding the transformation that happened in Vivekananda's life can help in awakening the ability to discern the Truth within you.

Narendra was born in Kolkata to Bhuvaneshwari Devi and Vishwanath Dutt. His father was an affluent lawyer. He had two more sons, other than Narendra. Narendra's grandfather Durgacharan had relinquished worldly life in his pursuit of God. While Narendra's mother was expecting him, she used to worship Lord Shiva to instil higher values in the unborn child. Little did she know that her son would grow up to be an ascetic mendicant. Later, when she learnt that her son aspired to become a monk, she was startled initially because she perceived it negatively. However, gradually she accepted it and even started feeling proud of it.

❑

2
Narendra's Courageous Childhood

That man has reached immortality who is disturbed by nothing material.

Narendra grew up to become a sweet, charming and an active boy. His mother had to take the services of two maids to control his unstoppable energy. When all other methods to pacify him failed, she would pour cold water over his head, chanting the name of Lord Shiva repeatedly and he would instantly calm down. Just as children have a natural affection for birds and animals, so did Narendra. His deep love for birds and animals was evident during the last phase of his life. Cows, monkeys, goats, peacocks, and some pigeons were his pets.

His mother played a crucial role in shaping his future. She became instrumental in the expression of his inherent qualities. One day, when Narendra returned home and complained that he was meted with an unfair treatment at school, his mother consoled him, "My son, don't despair. It was not your fault. Always follow the path of Truth without caring for the results. It is quite likely that while adhering to the Truth, sometimes you may have to face injustice and adverse consequences, but never abandon Truth at any cost." Not only did Narendra take note of his mother's advice, but after that, he also implemented it in his life. Another incident from his life confirms this fact.

Narendra was a master story-teller. His words were as magnetic as his personality. One day, while in school, he was narrating a story to his friends in the classroom. Everyone was listening to him with rapt attention. Suddenly, the teacher entered the classroom, and nobody came to know of it. The teacher was furious. He started asking questions on the subject to everyone, but only Narendra could answer them. The teacher spared him and asked all other students to stand on the bench as a punishment. Narendra knew that he was the culprit for his friends' punishment. So, he told the teacher, "I was narrating the story to my friends. Therefore, I should also be punished." Despite giving the right answers to all the questions, Narendra stood on the bench. This incident exemplifies how we should, under no circumstances, abandon the Truth. Truth has the power of winning the hearts of one and all.

Due to his extraordinary intelligence, soon Narendra drew the attention of his teachers and friends in school. Initially, he was not interested in learning English as it was a foreign language. But very soon, he became an expert in English. He used to finish his studies quickly and then spend most of his time in inventing new games and playing them. Along with this, Narendra also started a drama company and a gymnasium for children. He learnt sword fighting, wrestling and many other heroic games there. He was so restless that he would soon feel bored with one game and invent a new one. While playing, he would often resolve conflicts among other children. As a result, he became quite popular in his neighbourhood too. People used to praise his courage, honesty and simplicity.

There are some stories from his life, which describe his courageous nature. Reading them can awaken the fearless child within you.

***

As a child, once Narendra was playing a game of meditation with his friends. When it was his turn, he sat in meditation under a tree with his eyes closed. While he was completely immersed in meditation, his friends saw a cobra creep from the bushes and majestically sit before him. When he opened his eyes after some time, he saw the cobra seated before him. He just calmly smiled and replied, "I have only started practising meditation, and you have already come to compete with me on *Kundalini*. Go away! I will need some more time." Narendra's words cast a magical spell on the cobra, and the venomous serpent quietly turned away and disappeared into the bushes.

Narendra was fond of animals from his early childhood. He believed that if we love animals, they would never harm us. It was perhaps because of his kind and affectionate nature that the serpent did not harm him.

***

There is another incident from Narendra's life that describes his courageous nature. There was a *Peepal* tree in the courtyard of one of his neighbours. Narendra was very fond of climbing this tree. However, his neighbour was always worried that Narendra would fall from the tree and break his bones. The neighbour was also aware of Narendra's nature and knew that Narendra would never abstain from climbing the tree by merely asking him not to do so. Therefore, he devised another idea that would have worked on any ordinary child for sure. He warned Narendra, "A demon lives on this tree, and he does not like any child climbing on it. Therefore, if you want to be safe, stay away from this tree."

The neighbour thought that the mention of a demon on the tree would dissuade Narendra from climbing the tree and he would also remain safe. But he forgot that Narendra was no ordinary child. Soon after the neighbour left for his work, Narendra quickly climbed the tree and waited for the demon. An hour went by, then another, and soon it was evening. But the demon was nowhere in sight. In the meantime, the neighbour returned home. When Narendra saw him returning, he called out from the top of the tree, "Uncle, when would the demon come and strangle me? I have been waiting for him since morning, but now, I am tired." The poor neighbour asked Narendra to climb down from the tree and said, "Go, my dear child. Who would dare to frighten him, who is so courageous! The demon will not dare to come near you, but you must go home now and eat your food. It is evening, and you must be hungry."

Narendra was very intelligent and brave right from his childhood. He used to question the relevance of every rule, tradition, taboo and belief. If he was not satisfied with the answers, he would try it out on his own, and if the rule failed, he would never follow it.

***

Besides having a sharp mind, Narendra was also extremely courageous. Once, at the tender age of six years, he was returning home with his friends from somewhere. While walking by the roadside, unknowingly one of his friends started walking in the middle of the road. Suddenly, Narendra saw a horse-cart approaching his friend at high speed in the opposite direction. The boy was frightened and froze in the middle of the road, not knowing what to do. The cart had come very close to him, and the onlookers were certain that the child would surely get run over by the cart. But just then, Narendra, without wasting time, leapt towards him at lightning speed and dragged him to safety. People were all praises for the little Narendra for this heroic act and reported the entire incident to his mother. After hearing about her son's act of bravery, she was in tears. She hugged Narendra and said, "With God's grace, may you always help people in your life!"

Narendra was virtuous from his early childhood, and his mother was very proud of him. However, he was also very naughty, and his mother would sometimes get irritated with his behaviour and exclaim, "I had requested Lord Shiva to come to my house, but he has sent one of his demons instead!" In fact, Narendra was highly *rajasic* (the quality of dynamism and hyperactivity that expresses through the body-mind). A rajasic child cannot sit quietly and feels compelled to be active.

Despite this, whenever there was a discussion on the Ramayana or the Mahabharata at home, Narendra would sit and listen intently to the discussion. He was a devout devotee and also loved to meditate. People failed to understand how Narendra managed to sit still and meditate at such a tender age. They also wondered how he could sit quietly during the discussions held on the Ramayana and the Mahabharata, because sitting quietly was against his basic nature. People were surprised to see the sudden change in his behaviour, but nobody could comprehend what he was being prepared for. Although Narendra was predominantly rajasic, when it came to discussions on spiritual subjects, his *sattvic* qualities (qualities of piousness, balance and equanimity) used to prevail.

The childhood incidents from Swami Vivekananda's life are a source of inspiration for those parents who tend to be distressed with the rajasic behaviour of their children. If your child is hyperactive and can't sit quietly in one place, don't be worried about the child's future. Instead, let the child develop naturally. Whenever you feel tempted to worry about your child's future, simply recall the life of Swami Vivekananda – how he overcame the ill-effects of his rajasic nature with the help of his sattvic qualities.

In the further chapters, we will get to know of some incidents from Narendra's childhood that can encourage us to evoke the latent qualities within us.

❑

3
Intelligent Narendra

Condemn none; if you can stretch out a helping hand, do so. If you cannot, fold your hands, bless your brothers and let them go their own way.

In order to understand a person, it is important to look at his life holistically. There is no doubt that in his childhood Swami Vivekananda was very courageous and at the same time naughty too. However, the other side of the story is that he was equally good at studies.

Narendra had a sharp intellect. He could memorise his lessons in no time. He would then go along with his friends and play. His friends were baffled by his extraordinary capability and tried to imitate him. They also studied for a lesser time, but they had to repent because they couldn't mentally register and recall things in a short span of time like Narendra. They lacked that capability.

Many people were flabbergasted by this calibre of Narendra. There is an interesting episode about this aspect. It was the time when Narendra visited America after becoming the disciple of Ramakrishna Paramhansa. It so happened that Swami Vivekananda had to meet someone, so he reached the venue well in time. However, the other person was delayed. In the meanwhile, Swami Vivekananda picked up a book and started flipping through its pages.

After a short while, the person arrived, and their meeting started. During their talks, Swami Vivekananda referred to the same book that he was flipping through some time ago. The person astonishingly remarked, "Just now I noticed that you were merely flipping through the pages of that book, and now you are quoting references from it. How is this possible?" Swami Vivekananda calmly replied, "Anybody can do this by exercising complete control over his mind!"

Narendra acquired this ability with practice. Owing to his interest in a vast domain of knowledge, Narendra used to read books on all topics in his schooling years. Once he went to Raipur with his father for some days. He got a lot of spare time there. So, his father gave him a variety of books to read. His father was well aware of his son's fondness for books.

In Raipur, often many scholars used to visit Narendra's father. When they used to discuss history, spirituality, and literature, his father would ask Narendra to join him. By that time, Narendra had read almost all the works of famous Bengali writers and could also discuss on those books. The scholars used to be impressed with this ability of Narendra. In those gatherings, his father's friends used to remark that one day the young boy would raise Bengali literature to great heights. Narendra proved it true! After growing up, he wrote many famous Bengali books like, "Bartaman Bharat", "Parivrajaka", "Bhabbara Katha" and "Prachya O Paschatya".

In Narendra's life, the place of his parents was equivalent to that of his guru. The qualities that he imbibed from his parents helped him to become an eligible disciple of Ramakrishna Paramhansa. His mother always encouraged him to help others, and this inspired him to propagate the principle of universal brotherhood and universal humanity. His mother was also a courageous woman, and she always stood against any injustice and untruth with all her might.

On the one hand, Narendra's mother Bhuvaneshwari Devi affectionately instilled virtuous qualities in him and on the other hand, his father Vishwanath Dutt made him learn the lessons of self-control through discipline. It was his father's nature always to help people who approached him for any assistance as he was benevolent and kind. People would stay at his house for months together, and Narendra's father would bear their expenditure. This led to a situation that he could never save money for his family.

One day, Narendra was angry with his father and asked, "What would you leave behind for us?" At this, Vishwanath Dutt calmly replied, "Just get up and look into the mirror. You will see what I would leave behind." Narendra looked into the mirror. He saw his reflection and said, "Oh yes! I am there for myself. My father has made me capable enough to take care of myself." He understood what his father meant and never asked the question again.

Narendra's father was accustomed to living a luxurious life. Therefore, whatever he earned, he spent it for living on his terms and acquiring objects of luxury. Besides, Vishwanath Dutt always believed that he was the son of a poor recluse. The son of a poor man earns money, while the son of a prosperous man would lose his wealth. He never wanted that he should leave behind too much wealth that would pamper his sons and make them indolent and incompetent. Vishwanath Dutt was not an extravagant person and neither did he have any vices. He had a generous heart and used to spend freely for the benefit of the poor and the deserving. He was always an ideal for his son, Narendra.

Once, Narendra spoke rudely to his mother. In normal circumstances, any father would either punish or scold his son, but Vishwanath Dutt did not do so. That day, when Narendra's friends came to his house to play, they saw that his father had written on the door with a piece of coal, "Today, Narendra spoke rudely to his mother." This caused humiliation and extreme guilt in Narendra, and he decided to always speak carefully with everyone. It was for these reasons that Narendra had a lot of respect for his parents, and he was extremely proud of them. This also inculcated a feeling of self-respect in him.

If someone ever made fun of him by calling him childish or ignorant, he would become furious. However, this was not because of his ego, as he harboured neither malice nor jealousy for anyone. When someone used to doubt his capability, his confidence in his capability used to infuriate him.

Being a brilliant student, he always maintained the position of a leader amongst his friends. He was also a great orator from his childhood. He had even delivered a speech in his school. One of his teachers was going to leave the school, and a farewell speech had to be delivered in his honour. However, none of the students agreed to do so because of Surendranath Banerjee, a great orator and the chief guest, was present on the stage. No child could gather the courage to speak in his presence. Then, Narendra came forward and gave a wonderful speech in English for almost half an hour. It was his first speech. He delivered it with such courage and confidence that not only were his classmates and teachers impressed, but Surendranath Banerjee was also moved. That first speech of Narendra was a little preparation for the grand act that would ensue during the Parliament of World's Religions.

Besides participating in eloquence competitions and studies, Narendra also excelled in sports. He was very fond of wrestling and was a regular attendee at the gymnasium since the age of sixteen. He also won many awards in boxing and cricket. Likewise, he also practised music and earned a lot of praise for the devotional songs he would sing.

The kind of confidence and mental and physical strength that he developed by participating in such activities helped him to give a strong message to the world: "It is a sin to be weak, and one should try to get rid of it."

His all-round development took place in the company of Ramakrishna Paramhansa, and he became an inspiration for the youth. He inspired the youth to become fearless and courageous. These qualities of Swami Vivekananda helped him to become an exemplary disciple and a great human being.

❑

4

Million Dollar Questions by Curious Narendra

We are what our thoughts have made us; so take care of what you think. Words are secondary. Thoughts live; they travel far.

There was a temple of Lord Rama in a village. The temple priest used to serve with utmost devotion. After some days, news spread in the village that the priest had a glimpse of Lord Hanuman. Initially, villagers thought that it was just a rumour, but soon the news spread to other villages far and wide. People started flocking to the temple in large numbers. The villagers wondered that if the news was true then they too should benefit from it.

Everyone was quite excited by merely thinking about having a glimpse of Lord Hanuman. Some people even asked the priest, "We heard that you had seen Lord Hanuman. We too want to have a glimpse of Him. Can we also have that opportunity? Is it possible?"

The priest replied, "Yes, it is possible. But, Lord Hanuman comes only when the story of Lord Rama is narrated. Therefore, it would be good to organise such a program, and when Lord Hanuman visits this place, you can catch His glimpse." The villagers liked his suggestion. They collected money and organised the program on a grand scale. People from faraway places came to attend the program.

It is believed that Lord Hanuman was granted a boon that wherever discourses on the story of Lord Rama were organised, he would get a chance to listen to them. Be it anytime or age; He would never be deprived of it.

As suggested by the priest, the discourse was organised wherein all kinds of people, rich and poor, sages and saints came to attend the program. During the discourse, holy *prasad* (religious offering that is consumed by worshippers after the worship) was distributed amongst the devotees. A little away from that place, some lepers were sitting under a tree and were waiting for their turn to get the prasad and to iisten to the story of Lord Rama. Amongst them, one leper was badly affected by the disease. Those who saw them harboured disgust and hatred for them and even avoided looking at them.

When the person distributing the prasad saw the lepers, he told the others, "These lepers seem to be hungry. Let us distribute prasad to them as well." However, some people stopped him and said, "What are you doing? Let us first distribute the prasad to all the great people who have assembled here. We must first make arrangements for them. If any prasad is left after that, we can give it to these lepers too. It shouldn't happen that we fall short of prasad if we distribute it to these lepers first."

Finally, the discourse was over late at night. The prasad was distributed to one and all. Everyone happily participated in it.

The next day, those people who wanted to catch a glimpse of Lord Hanuman, went to the priest and complained, "You said that we would get a glimpse of Lord Hanuman during the discourse, but no such thing happened."

The priest calmly replied, "Lord Hanuman had indeed graced us with his presence, but you did not recognise him."

People were taken aback by his reply and asked, "Where was Lord Hanuman? We didn't see Him anywhere."

The priest then revealed the secret, "A few lepers were seated under the tree. The one, who was the most severely affected of them all, to whom you did not give the prasad, was Lord Hanuman! You must first learn to recognise Lord Hanuman as He can come in any form. Only then can you catch His glimpse and render service to Him. If you fail to, you will only keep presuming and imagining Him and can never get His real glimpse."

The moral of the story for the youth is that one must treat any opportunity as God-given and learn to recognise it. People get ample opportunities during their lifetime, but they fail to recognise them as opportunities. Once you learn to recognise opportunities in life, it raises your worthiness to attain the Truth.

Narendra was also in search of a similar opportunity because he was also very keen to have a glimpse of Lord Hanuman. But he never believed anything without proper evidence. Being inquisitive by nature, he used to have several questions in his mind.

If you ask the right question, at the right time, at the right place and in the right manner, you might not get only the answer, but you may also attain liberation. This is the power of questioning. Till now, whoever asked the right questions has attained liberation. The questions, which are capable of awakening and liberating you are called million-dollar questions. Calling them million-dollar questions denotes their worth so that one can differentiate them from trivial or mundane questions.

A million-dollar question is so-called so that a person can differentiate between a right question, a wrong question and a million-dollar question. Million-dollar questions can lead to liberation from ignorance and awakening of true wisdom. By persistently questioning "Who am I now?" you can get liberated from false beliefs and thoughts. You can unshackle yourself from the idea that you are the body.

Million dollar questions show one the right path, help him in making the right choices in his life and lead him on the path to enlightenment. For this reason, these questions are invaluable and powerful. Narendra had such million dollar questions burning within him right from his childhood. Let's learn about them in detail now.

Is it possible to meet Lord Hanuman?

The mythological epic, Ramayana, explains how the mortal lives of each of its characters came to an end, except that of Lord Hanuman. There is no mention of the mortal body of Hanuman. When Narendra heard about the character of Lord Hanuman in the Ramayana during his childhood, a million dollar question occurred to him, "Is Lord Hanuman still alive? Is He immortal? If yes, how can I meet Him?" When Narendra was told that it is not possible to meet Lord Hanuman, he asked, "Why is it not possible? If He is indeed alive, then He must be present somewhere, and I should be able to meet Him."

Narendra had also heard that Lord Hanuman always visits those places where the story of Lord Rama is narrated. Hence, he visited all such places and asked people, "Would Lord Hanuman visit this place? I also want to meet Him." This incident indicates how curious and earnest he was to find the Truth at such a tender age. These are the characteristics of a true seeker of Truth.

Another incident regarding Narendra's curiosity about religion shows that he never believed anything without evidence. Narendra's father Vishwanath Dutt was an advocate. Whenever he used to win court cases for his clients, the clients used to bring sweets to his house. Some of his clients were Muslims. When they used to gift sweets, no one used to eat them. Due to orthodox misbeliefs in society during those times, eating food served by a Muslim was not considered appropriate by high-caste Hindus. When Narendra heard about it, he decided to find the Truth himself. Therefore, one day he relished the sweets brought by a Muslim client but did not suffer any adverse effects that his family members were apprehensive of. While he was eating sweets, his family members observed him in utter dismay, considering it to be blasphemous. But Narendra understood that these were all misconceptions created by the human mind, and there was no truth in them.

Have you seen God?

Because of his sharp intellect, Narendra always thought logically. In his journey of search for God, with the passage of time, he first became a wayfarer, then a seeker. After that, he took the form of a disciple, who later transformed into a true devotee. He expressed the divine qualities of the Self by being a true devotee.

In his journey of Truth, when he was a wayfarer, he was searching for Truth at different places, in different schools of spirituality. It was the time of his student life. Whenever any preachers visited his city, he met them. He was so inquisitive that he would directly ask them, "Have you seen God?" They were taken aback as nobody had asked them such direct questions, ever before.

Many preachers and prophets of different religions visited the city of Kolkata, but none could answer Narendra in the affirmative. Despite that, he continued to meet them and ask the same question repeatedly. It was another million dollar question!

After some time, in his quest for God, Narendra got associated with a spiritual organisation named Brahmo Samaj and became its member. There he practised music, singing devotional songs. Whenever any religious preachers visited that place, Narendra would ask them the same question, "Have you seen God?" They were either dumbstruck or used to blabber. Narendra became clear that he would not get his answer there.

It was not that he was satisfied by joining the Brahmo Samaj, but till a person attains his desired objective, he continues to do something or the other for achieving it. The same was the case with Narendra. He was a wayfarer, wandering in search of God and was seeking an answer to his question. Since no preacher from any religion could answer his question, soon, he became restless. He thought, "There must be at least one person on this earth, who must have seen God." He wanted to meet that person.

One day, Narendra happened to meet Maharshi Debendranath Thakur. Those days, Maharshi was living in a boat on the shore of a river and engaging in his spiritual practice there. When Narendra came to know of him, he reached the place out of curiosity and started asking him questions. He answered many of his questions, but Narendra said, "I just need the answer to one question: Have you seen God?" Maharshi replied, "You have got a brilliant spark in your eyes and your physical traits also resemble that of a yogi. If you earnestly pray to God, call upon Him, engage in spiritual practice, you will surely attain Him." This reply deeply touched Narendra and transformed him from a wayfarer into an earnest seeker. The difference between a wayfarer and a seeker is that the former visits different places to find something, whereas a seeker attains his objective by being rooted to the same place. The search for the guru ends only when one becomes a seeker.

After becoming a seeker, Narendra's way of life changed to that of a yogi. He began to wear white clothes and stayed alone in a rented house. His family members thought that he wanted to stay in seclusion so that it would not affect his studies. His father always gave him ample freedom. Hence nobody stopped him from doing so. He began sleeping on the floor like a yogi and gradually renounced all the luxuries of life.

He would read religious books in the time that he could afford after his studies and practice of music. He would discuss only religious topics with his friends. Thus, his life changed completely after meeting Maharshi Debendranath Thakur. He was raising his worthiness to attain God. He was in search of a true master, who was soon to come in his life. It is said that when a disciple is completely ready to acquire knowledge, the guru has to come in his life to fulfil his life purpose.

❑

5

Narendra's Thirst to Realize God

To advance, we must have faith in ourselves first and then in God. He who has no faith in himself can never have faith in God.

If you set out on a mission to attain success, all your relatives encourage you. When you strive to master an art, your friends and teachers support you. If you are aspiring to become Miss India or Miss universe, many people will applaud you, but nobody would appreciate you in your quest for God. It is the path on which you will have to tread alone. When Narendra set out in search of God, people began to consider him crazy. However, one of his distant relatives, Dr. Ramchandra Dutt, who was his good friend, encouraged Narendra to move ahead on this path as he understood him well.

As soon as Narendra had finished his B.A. exams, his family started looking out for a suitable match for him. When his father tried to pursue the matrimonial case further, he refused because he was not at all interested in getting married. He was in search of the ultimate Truth.

Narendra spoke his mind to Dr. Ramchandra, "Brother! I do not want to get married because marriage is not my requirement. Instead, it is just contrary to my objective in life."

Ramchandra listened to Narendra intently. By gazing into his eyes, he enquired, "Then what is your goal of life? Is getting a higher education, or obtaining name and fame, or reforming the society or striving to make your country independent?"

Narendra said, "No! My only objective is to realise God. I do not require any life partner for myself. Instead, I only need the company of God. I request you to kindly explain to my father that I view every woman as my mother and it is not possible for me to look at women in any other manner."

Ramchandra was taken aback by Narendra's reply. He tried to explain, "So many people get married, they have children and rear them. They also go to temples, worship God and get blessed. Likewise, you can also get married and continue your pursuit of God while also leading a married life." Narendra replied, "People go to the temple, only to get Prasad, not God! I want to attain God. I wish to attain the Almighty just as the seekers described in our scriptures have. Please understand my feelings and talk to my father in my favour."

Ramchandra Dutt smiled at Narendra and patted his shoulder, "If you wish to get rid of the worldly entanglements and realise God by your own choice, then take refuge of Ramakrishna Paramhansa from Dakshineshwar. He is the right person to show you the correct path. I also visit him for wisdom." This was the second incident, which proved to be a turning point in Narendra's life.

Narendra came in contact with Ramakrishna Paramhansa, and his life underwent a major transformation. People normally remember the Almighty only when they are in trouble. But Narendra was eager to attain God despite having all the comforts and conveniences of life.

A seeker of Truth must have a strong internal urge – "All this while, I was ignorant about the ultimate Truth. But now that I have become aware of it, I cannot hold myself away from it. Now, I must attain the ultimate Truth." When the seeker of Truth is ready in this manner, he does not get entangled in the external appearance, costume, or age of the guru. When there is an earnest desire within a seeker to attain God, he single-mindedly pays attention to the ultimate Truth, nothing else.

If you succeed to ignore these external factors and attain the ultimate Truth, then you will truly benefit from it. By obtaining this benefit, you will rise above all gains and losses, and get liberated from them. However, it calls for the earnest thirst for Truth and true love for freedom.

If you have the same kind of thirst for the attainment of God, as Narendra had, you would also find the path extremely simple, straightforward and accessible. The most important step towards finding the ultimate Truth is to develop eagerness, because unless one is eager enough, one is likely to get entangled in external factors. When intense thirst for the Truth arises within a seeker, he longs to abide in the Truth alone, in the present moment, regardless of the place, time or surroundings that he is in.

When the thirst for realising the Truth intensifies, the quest is transformed into the spontaneous, effortless effort. Narendra had also developed such a craving for Truth. Men of his age were getting married and settling into their domestic lives, but Narendra was obsessed with the desire of realising God. He was eager to experience God and attain Him. Time and again, he would pray –

"Now, I want God, and God alone.
I will be satisfied only when I find Him.
No mundane thing in this world can satiate my thirst now.
I have wandered enough after worldly affairs,
I have pursued the materialistic world in vain.
The topics and objects of the world cannot quench my thirst.
If I attain you, I will be satisfied.
You alone can satiate my thirst."

When the heart calls out to God with such an affectionate longing, it takes the form of a real prayer and leads one to the attainment of God. It was this intense thirst and eagereness in Narendra that caused his accorded guru to appear in his life.

❑

PART – 2

The Ganga of Wisdom comes to the Doorstep

6

A Melodious Disciple meets his Harmonious Guru

Truth can be stated in a thousand different ways, yet each one can be true.

In the divine play of the guru-disciple relationship, one was melodious, and the other was harmonious. Vivekananda had excellent knowledge of music, and he used to sing hymns melodiously. Ramakrishna Paramhansa always insisted Vivekananda sing devotional songs. Upon listening to his soulful songs, the master would slip into a state of trance. The master was harmonious because his human state was fully in harmony with the divinity within him. This is why one was known to express musical melody, and the other was regarded as the epitome of divine harmony.

In those days, there were various spiritual sects and their organisations. Brahmo Samaj was one of these organisations where Swami Vivekananda used to visit and also sing before he got acquainted with Ramakrishna Paramhansa. He was appreciated a lot for his singing there. Later, he started singing during the discourses of Ramakrishna Paramhansa. As he started gaining understanding from Ramkrishna Paramhansa, gradually the nature of songs sung by him also changed. In the beginning, one usually sings popular songs. However, when one acquires true wisdom, one is no more restricted within the confines of popular songs. The internalised wisdom begins to express itself in the form of songs.

Any task is possible only when there is a perfect attunement with it. If you want to earn health, wealth, prosperity, have good relations, get a good life partner and good children, but if you think negatively and with pessimism, then your mental state is not attuned with what you aspire. This would cause obstacles in your path.

Ramakrishna Paramhansa always abided in divine harmony. He was always attuned to divinity. His attention was completely and unremittingly focused on the purpose for which he had taken birth. Therefore, everything was going along perfectly as per his divine plan. There was a magnetic attraction between the melodious disciple and his attuned master. This is why sometimes Narendra would be attracted towards his guru and at times the other way round.

The evening on the festive day of Durga Puja served as the pretext for their meeting. The canopy was brightly lit, and devotees had started coming in large numbers. Musicians were readying their musical instruments for singing religious songs. Narendra and his friend Ravi sat near the group of singers. On account of his regular singing in the Brahmo Samaj, Narendra had developed an interest in singing, and he also had a melodious voice. When the program started, Narendra also joined in.

Narendra's singing spellbound people. The other singers also appreciated his singing and gradually, his popularity spread. After a few days of this incident, Narendra's neighbour Surendranath invited Ramakrishna Paramhansa to his house and organised a function. He had heard a lot about Narendra's singing proficiency, so he invited Narendra for the function.

Narendra sang a song, which touched Ramakrishna Paramhansa deeply. He was listening to the song intently. When the song ended, he called Ramchandra Dutt and said, "Bring this boy to me at Dakshineshwar." Narendra also heard this.

Before leaving, Thakur (as Ramakrishna Paramhansa was popularly known) stopped near Narendra. He took both his hands in his own, looked intently at them as if he was searching for something and then said, "You sing very well. You have come to this world for the welfare of society. You are not an ordinary human. Come to Dakshineshwar and seek the blessings of Goddess Kali. Will you come, Narendra?"

This was the first meeting between Narendra and Ramakrishna Paramhansa. Narendra was merely eighteen years old then. Narendra came to know that people better knew Ramakrishna Paramhansa as Thakur, but his behaviour appeared somewhat awkward to Narendra. Surendranath had only called him to sing a song and being his neighbour, Narendra had agreed to it. However, he was wondering why this topic of visiting Dakshineshwar was mooted. He kept looking at Thakur in amazement. Thakur once again insisted him to visit Dakshineshwar. Finally, he nodded in agreement.

Surendranath was a great devotee of Ramakrishna Paramhansa. He explained many aspects of Ramakrishna Paramhansa's life to Narendra in detail.

Ramakrishna Paramhansa had come to Kolkata from a very small village, Kamarpukur from the district of Hugali, in search of employment. However, he felt contented and fulfilled at the feet of Goddess Kali. Therefore, he abandoned the idea of employment and became the priest of Goddess Kali temple.

The state of ecstasy that he used to slip into in front of Goddess Kali was not the result of any spiritual austerity or practice. He had, in fact, experienced that state at the age of six years. At a time when children of his age went to school, Ramakrishna was immersed in devotion and would sing hymns in the fields. This was the temperament at his home too. His father was a poor Brahmin, but no sage who visited Kamarpukur would ever return hungry from his house. Ramakrishna was also, therefore, in the habit of serving the saints. He would also sit with them and listen to their discussions about God and spirituality.

Once Ramakrishna bade farewell to a group of saints and was returning home while melodiously singing a hymn. Suddenly he looked at the sky and felt a strange sense of emptiness in his mind. He closed his eyes and sat under a tree. It was a moment when Ramakrishna experienced the state of *Samadhi* for the first time in his life. He was merely six years old then. After the demise of his father, the conditions at home became very difficult. He had to accompany his elder brother to Kolkata for earning a livelihood. His elder brother was a learned Brahmin who used to run a small school in Kolkata.

Being simple and honest, Ramakrishna very soon realised that he would derive no benefit out of this materialistic knowledge. He asked himself, "What is the use of such knowledge, by which I am unable to abide in God?" He wanted to return to his village immediately but could not do so. His elder brother proposed that he should go to Dakshineshwar and accept the role of a priest in the temple of Goddess Kali. Ramakrishna gladly agreed.

While worshipping the goddess, he would reflect upon the Lord of the universe in the form of Goddess Kali. He had a strong desire to have a vision of God and every day he would pray to the Goddess, "O Mother, today, again, I could not get your glimpse." Several days and months passed by. One day, finally he had a divine vision of Goddess Kali. From that day onwards, he started promoting and propagating the knowledge of enlightenment and spiritual practice to people for attaining that state. He would talk to everyone visiting Dakshineshwar temple, regardless of their religion and caste. In this way, he gained the knowledge of religions like Islam and Christianity.

Ramakrishna Paramhansa would remain absorbed in divine ecstasy. He would sit and listen to divine songs and enter a state of trance. He would enter that state even merely by hearing anyone saying, "Jai Mata or Jai Sri Ram!" His disciples were often worried that he might slip into the state of trance, even while walking on the road. Therefore, they used to take extra care of their master.

A person attains the state of ecstasy when he is too engrossed in a particular topic even to take note of his physical body. Just as a blotting paper absorbs ink completely, when a person enters the state of Samadhi, he loses the sense of his mortal body. He even does not realise if some harm has been caused to the body. Ramakrishna Paramhansa was in such a state of divine bliss.

When the disciple is ready, the guru has to appear in his life. Narendra had become a matured disciple, and therefore, Ramakrishna Paramhansa appeared in his life as his master. Initially, Narendra was unable to recognise him as his guru. But gradually, he realised the Truth and then became his devout disciple.

Narendra was a rational person, but due to the blessings of his master, his life transformed. It was impossible to consider Ramakrishna Paramhansa and Vivekananda separately, just as it is impossible to consider the sun separately from its rays. The duo had become one, like the sun and its rays. The arrival of Ramakrishna Paramhansa in Swami Vivekananda's life is a momentous incident, which exemplifies the ideal relationship between a master and a disciple.

❑

7

Alert Disciple, Focused Guru

This world is the great gymnasium where we come to make ourselves strong.

Ramkrishna Paramhansa's life was always centred in the divine essence. It is because of this essence that the meaning and purpose of his life unfolded. He remained absorbed in the fulfilment of his purpose all through his life. Narendra, on the other hand, was proficient in all subjects and was a very alert student. He used to minutely examine everything very closely, big or small, irrespective of the time it took to do so. For the same reason, he would get into the depth of everything and learn all aspects of it.

When Narendra met Ramakrishna Paramhansa, he was equally alert as he used to be in the class. He was fully attentive to all the aspects including what kind of people came to meet Ramakrishna Paramhansa, what questions they asked, what answers the master gave them and what the other people were doing around him. Narendra would observe everything very minutely. Whatever Ramakrishna preached, Narendra examined that too.

After his first meeting with Ramakrishna Paramhansa, Narendra once again went to Dakshineshwar to meet him. During his first meeting, he could not converse with Thakur, but could only see him. Therefore, he felt the urge to meet his master once again. He went to see Thakur with his million dollar question.

In his second meeting, without losing any time, Narendra asked him, "Have you seen God?" To this, the master replied, "Yes, indeed! Just as I see you, so have I seen God in the same manner and have also talked to God. If you also want to see God, you too can do so."

These days, people do not consider knowing God. If someone's spouse dies, or anyone from the family passes away, they cry bitterly. But nobody grieves over the fact that they have not been able to see God yet. The truth is that only those, who grieve for God, realise him!

Finally, Narendra had received a confident answer to his question. Ramakrishna Paramhansa claimed, "I have seen God, and I can also get you to see Him." Narendra did not believe him easily because his intellect dominated his acceptance of what was being said. The second meeting of Narendra with Ramakrishna Paramhansa was memorable. Many more such meetings were to happen. This was just the beginning.

Seeing the illogical behaviour of Ramakrishna Paramhansa, Narendra felt as if Ramakrishna Paramhansa knew him since ages.

On that day, Ramakrishna Paramhansa made Narendra sit beside him and sing a devotional song. While Narendra sang, Thakur went into a state of trance. After the song was over, Thakur held his hand and brought him out into the courtyard and pleaded, "Why did you take so long to come here? How could you remain away from me for such a long time?" He became emotional, and tears welled up in his eyes.

He continued, "I had been waiting for you since so long. I am fed up with listening to the worthless talks of people. Now that you have come, it would give me immense pleasure to talk to a true seeker. You are Narayana in the guise of a common man (Nara). You have taken birth for the welfare of humanity."

Usually, most of the people who came to see Ramakrishna Paramhansa urged him, "I have these domestic problems... I am suffering from this mental trauma... If I get the blessings of Mother Kali, I will be freed from these problems." Usually, people approach a temple priest with such futile issues. There were only a few who had a genuine interest in knowing the Truth. Narendra did not do anything extraordinary. In the presence of Ramakrishna Paramhansa, he had only sung a few songs which he had learnt at Brahmo Samaj. But merely by listening to his songs, Ramakrishna Paramhansa came to know of the purity of Narendra's heart.

Narendra was however perplexed with the remarks of Ramakrishna Paramhansa. He wondered, "Look whom I have come to meet! (Is he in his senses?) I am Vishwanath Dutt's son. I am an ordinary person. But Ramakrishna Paramhansa regards me as God, who has just now descended from heaven!"

While Narendra was lost in his thoughts, Ramakrishna suddenly approached him. He had butter, candies and sweets in his hand. He tried to feed Narendra with his hands and said, "Have it, my child." Narendra held his hand and tried to stop him. He said, "Kindly give me the sweets. I will share them with my friends. I do not like eating it alone."

Ramakrishna said, "They would also eat, but first you have it." Thus Ramakrishna continued to feed him the sweets and Narendra helplessly had them. After that, he took Narendra with him inside the room and appreciated him in front of everybody, "Look, how brilliant Narendra appears in the radiance of his knowledge." Everyone who was present looked with amazement at Narendra.

While Ramakrishna was appreciating Narendra, Narendra's logical mind was caught in a dilemma. He felt that Ramakrishna would give some special message, some sermon or teaching, but whatever he was saying sounded futile to Narendra.

Narendra noticed that Ramakrishna Paramhansa was talking a few minutes illogically back, and now he was meeting others as if nothing had happened. Narendra was perplexed to see this unnatural behaviour of Ramakrishna Paramhansa and wondered, "Is he some saint or a lunatic?"

While Narendra was taking leave of Ramakrishna, he was allowed to leave only on the condition that he would soon come back. Narendra somehow managed to wriggle out, thinking that he had met some crazy person.

Narendra kept thinking about it for many days. His mind was tired of analysing the peculiar behaviour and remarks of Ramakrishna Paramhansa. He tried to forget everything that had happened to him and resolved not to go back to meet Ramakrishna again, but it did not happen so. Narendra remained associated with Brahmo Samaj and also visited Dakshineshwar time and again. Gradually he was attracted to the childlike innocence and unpretentious personality, the sweet words and unconditional love of Ramakrishna Paramhansa.

This is how the attraction builds up between the guru and the disciple. When two things are opposites in nature, they develop an ultimate attraction between them. When a person asking for the greatest of attainments comes before the biggest benefactor, what kind of a relationship and attraction can develop between them? Though this is not always so in all kinds of opposite relationships.

In the guru-disciple relationship, where one is giving the Truth, and the latter is asking for the Truth, the attraction is equally strong at both the ends. Hence, it is termed as the most important relationship of all. It is a relationship that transcends all other worldly relations. It takes a considerable time to understand it. When one understands the purport of the guru-disciple relationship, one gets liberated from all suffering and illusion.

Narendra was determined on realising the Truth. When he came across the greatest benefactor and a wise guru in the form of Ramakrishna Paramhansa, Truth was revealed in his life. Ramakrishna Paramhansa always saw a divine presence in Narendra. Hence he loved him so dearly. He wanted Narendra to experience the same absolute bliss that he had experienced. He wanted to break Narendra's habit of riding on two boats. A true master neither tries to please his disciple like a political leader does to the public to garner votes nor does he expect any material gains from his disciple. This is because the real master transcends all worldly gains and losses.

In the beginning, it is natural for a disciple to have doubts about the guru or his knowledge. It is difficult to convey Truth in words, but the guru still tries to explain it in simple words for us. It is for this reason that sometimes the master talks illogically or behaves unconventionally. This confuses the disciple because he is unable to understand his master's behaviour or words. However, it is in the disciple's best interest to always have faith that there is a reason behind the master's behaviour. The master reveals the secrets to his disciple at the right time.

A disciple ought to give importance to everything that the master says, even if it sounds humorous or careless because a real master never says anything futile. Otherwise, the disciple can get confused and cause harm to oneself. A disciple should never make the mistake of listening to the mind and ignoring the directions of the master. The words spoken by the master are like prophecy. They are golden words. A true disciple understands the value and importance of the teachings of the guru. He knows that the words spoken by the guru are not mere words. Hence he listens to them like a prophecy. He knows that whatever the master speaks, should be meditated and reflected upon. True reflection then starts the journey towards the Truth.

The guru often examines whether the disciple has full faith in him. The master reveals the ultimate Truth only when the disciple develops complete faith in him. The ultimate Truth liberates the disciple from all the illusions of the world. It is the master who leads the disciple into the state of enlightenment. When the disciple understands the working of his guru, all his doubts get eradicated, and he realises the true essence of the guru principle.

The guru speaks to the one who-we-truly-are, not the limited individual persona that we have believed ourselves to be. He does not speak to please us, but he awakens us with his unconditional love and wisdom.

The guru guides his disciple from the head to the heart. Initially, the disciple analyses everything using his intellect, but after meeting the guru, he learns to stay in the heart beyond all reasoning. When he gains understanding, he makes all his decisions from his heart. After coming in contact with Ramakrishna Paramhansa, Narendra also got the opportunity to shift his focus from head to heart.

❑

8
Narendra's First Experience of Samadhi

The more we come out and do good to others,
the more our hearts will be purified, and God will be in them.

Very soon, Ramakrishna Paramhansa made Narendra experience a glimpse of the state of Samadhi. Narendra did not know what Samadhi meant. To attain the state of Samadhi, you need to be attuned to it.

Samadhi is the state that transcends time; it is the state of consciousness before the time came into existence. Samadhi is the state of knowing the experience that exists before the world came into existence. The concept of time came much later. The measurement of time started from the moment the world came into being. Being in the timeless state of wakefulness, which is beyond mind, body and intellect is known as Samadhi.

The state that exists beyond time and space is known as Samadhi. It is the state, where we meet the creator. The creator exists within us. True spirituality is knowing the existence of the creator. We are actually in the state of Samadhi while in a deep sleep, but we are not aware of the number of hours that passed while we are asleep. It is only after we wake up and look at the time that we can make out how many hours we were asleep. Every night, we are in the state of Samadhi, but this Samadhi happens in the state of unconsciousness.

The state of Samadhi can be experienced in waking state. But for that, the disciple needs to prepare himself and become worthy. Swami Vivekananda had the first experience of Samadhi when he was not at all prepared for it.

Once, Narendra went to Dakshineshwar with some of his friends. Ramakrishna Paramhansa was sitting in the temple. As soon as he saw Narendra, he asked him to sit near him. When the singing of devotional songs started, Narendra saw that Ramakrishna was advancing towards him. He had the apprehension that probably Ramakrishna would start speaking incoherently as he had done before. But when Ramakrishna came very close to Narendra and placed his hand on his head, Narendra was instantaneously transported into an unknown state of blankness. That was Narendra's first experience of Samadhi. He experienced that all the objects were revolving around him and gradually vanishing.

Narendra was terrified with this experience. He felt as if he was nearing death. He gathered courage and asked, "What are you doing? I want to go back to my parents." Then Ramakrishna Paramhansa touched Narendra's heart and said, "Alright, let's not do this now. There is no hurry. This is enough for today." After that, Narendra emerged from the state of Samadhi.

It was a big jolt for Narendra. This happens with most people who experience Samadhi for the first time. They fail to understand what is happening to them in that state and get frightened. It is very easy for a frightened person to become a cause of trouble for himself as well as for others. Narendra was very proud of his fearless nature, but this experience shattered his pride.

Ramakrishna Paramhansa decided that he would first prepare Narendra for this experience so that after Narendra attains the state of Samadhi, he would be able to hold it properly and be established in it. Narendra had the habit of assessing everything using his intellect. He had passed all the examinations in his college and had a very sharp and logical brain. Given this, how could he understand the experience of Samadhi, which is beyond the reasoning ability of the human intellect? Hence, he got frightened when he entered that state.

Just as a farmer prepares the soil before sowing seeds, a true master also prepares his disciple for imparting true wisdom. A farmer does not sow the seeds directly into the soil. If the soil is rocky, then he first removes all the stones. Then he removes the weeds and other wild vegetation. After that, he waters the soil to make it soft. Once the soil becomes soft, he digs it to sow the seeds.

Ramakrishna Paramhansa also wanted to prepare Narendra in the same manner before giving him true knowledge. He was able to see the latent qualities in Narendra, and he knew that Narendra would utilise his knowledge and experience for the welfare of people.

At that time, Narendra was not ready for experiencing Samadhi, but Ramakrishna knew that a disciple receives whatever he is eligible for. For example, when someone says, "I am unable to get a job" then he is asked, "Are you ready for the job?" It is the law of nature that the more prepared you are, the bigger opportunities come your way. Once you are prepared, no power can stop you from getting a good job. Therefore, until you get a job, you must prepare your mind and body for it. Increase your skill set, raise your capabilities, work on the art of time management and enhance your concentration. Learn whatever is necessary before getting the job.

If one needs to prepare himself so much for getting an ordinary job, then we can very well imagine how much preparation Ramakrishna Paramhansa would have made for Narendra, so that he could attain the state of Samadhi.

Narendra had not been able to understand the experience of Samadhi, but after that first experience, he started reflecting on his experience. Initially, he felt that probably Ramakrishna

Paramhansa had hypnotised him. Since Narendra was a student of the Arts faculty, he had studied Psychology and also had adequate knowledge of the subject. Despite this, he was in a dilemma and asked himself, "On one side you say that Ramakrishna Paramhansa is a lunatic and on the other side, you claim that he can hypnotise you. Both these statements are contradictory. On one side you say that he looks like a saint and on the other side, you say that he behaves awkwardly because he is muddle-headed. Perhaps for the same reason, he speaks to Mother Kali and goes into a trance." The truth was that Narendra couldn't comprehend his first experience of Samadhi. Man is blessed from the beginning, but he is not able to understand it then.

After a week, Narendra visited Ramakrishna Paramhansa again. Ramakrishna addressed everyone present there and said, "Narendra is an extraordinary person, and he has many virtues. Everybody should respect him." Ramakrishna used to praise Narendra so much that he would often feel surprised. Sometimes Ramakrishna would say, "Narendra is one of the sages from the seven stars (*Saptarshi*) in the sky. At other times, he would say, "Narendra is a sword, which has come out of its scabbard."

Ramakrishna often said about Narendra, "Look, how brilliant a student he is! He studies so well and talks so politely. He has mastery of music. He is amazing. No one can have so many qualities at the same time! He is good in studies and also does exceptionally well in religious discussions. There is no one to match Narendra."

Ramakrishna Paramhansa had made several rules for other disciples but treated Narendra as an exception to all those rules. He would say, "It does not matter whether Narendra follows the rules or not. Rules are made for immature people. Narendra is fully mature, and he does not need any rules." All these words made Narendra wonder what Ramakrishna was foreseeing in him. He considered himself to be an ordinary person, even after having his first experience of Samadhi.

It was a time when many things were happening in Narendra's life. On the one hand, his family members were discussing getting him married. On the other hand, he had extraordinary spiritual experiences. He was also worried about his future, and he often mulled about the path that he should take.

❑

9
The Love between Master and Disciple

The visible persona is merely a manifestation of the invisible mindset.

Thakur loved Narendra immensely and wanted him to visit Dakshineshwar every day. He was his favourite disciple, and he longed to meet him. At times, when Narendra would not visit him for a few days, he would send somebody to Kolkata to call for Narendra. Once, Ramakrishna Paramhansa asked Narendra to visit him, but despite his repeated requests, Narendra could not find the time. Ramakrishna knew that Narendra used to sing devotional songs at the Brahmo Samaj. Therefore, he decided to go there to meet Narendra.

It was evening. The devotees of Brahmo Samaj of Kolkata had gathered there, and their meeting was in process. All of a sudden Thakur entered the place. People, who were sitting there, became excited to get his glimpse. As Thakur approached the dais and looked at Narendra, he entered the state of Samadhi. Narendra sensed that the leaders of the Brahmo Samaj might not have liked the sudden and unplanned arrival of Ramakrishna Paramhansa, so nobody came forward to welcome him. In fact, some people tried to ignore him. Narendra did not like this humiliation of his master.

There was chaos in the gathering as everybody wanted to see the man in the state of Samadhi. To control the crowd, one

Brahmo Samaj leader extinguished all gas lights in the hall, but there was complete mayhem because of the darkness that prevailed. Narendra quickly embraced Thakur to save him from the stampede. In that commotion, Thakur emerged from the state of Samadhi. Narendra could not leave Thakur in that state alone, so he accompanied him to Dakshineshwar. After this incident, Narendra developed a newfound affection for Thakur.

In another similar incident, when Thakur could not bear Narendra's separation for long, he went to Kolkata to meet Narendra. He was told that Narendra was studying with his classmate in a room on the second floor of his house. The stairs of the house were quite high. Therefore two people helped Thakur reach Narendra's room. As soon as he entered the room, he entered the state of Samadhi. Narendra's classmate enquired with utter surprise, "Who is this gentleman?" Narendra replied, "You may go home now. We will study together some other time."

In fact, Narendra also felt affection for Thakur, but he seldom expressed it. He used to ridicule Thakur's spiritual stability as the lack of self-control, and he would also belittle Thakur for worshipping Goddess Kali.

Once Ramakrishna asked Narendra, "When you do not have faith in my goddess, why do you come here?"

Narendra replied, "I do not come here for Goddess Kali, but I come here for you. I like to listen to your words of wisdom."

On another day, there was a similar argument between Thakur and Narendra. Narendra became very aggressive. However, Thakur did not approve any of Narendra's arguments. He kept nodding his head in disagreement. Finally, Narendra started ignoring even Thakur's statements. He sat sulkily as if every word spoken by Thakur was pinching him. Despite this, Thakur lovingly made him understand the point. This shows the unshakable bond of love between the guru and his disciple.

Many times their banter would make the atmosphere jovial. Once, while adjusting his *Tanpura* (a stringed musical instrument), Narendra jokingly asked Thakur, "Do you know that it takes a long time to setup the Tanpura and tune it?"

Ramakrishna Paramhansa replied, "Now, he would strum it for a while."

Some other disciple mocked, "The Tanpura would be set today and singing of devotional songs can happen only tomorrow."

At this, Ramakrishna Paramhansa said, "We should break open this Tanpura." In this way, sometimes everybody used to make fun of Narendra. Narendra would then retort, "Those people, who are ignorant of music, are free to make such loose comments!"

At this Ramakrishna Paramhansa replied, "Look, he defeated all at once with one simple reply."

Such conversations reflected the mutual love between the master and his disciple.

Ramakrishna Paramhansa never stressed upon Narendra that he was his guru. He also never instructed Narendra to snap his ties with the Brahmo Samaj. Thakur granted him full liberty to choose the way he was progressing in his life and didn't hurry him to learn everything quickly. The love showered by the guru is that of wisdom. This love of the guru, which is imbued with wisdom, bestows the intellect with the power of discerning the Truth. It blesses the mind with sublime devotion, which ultimately leads to liberation. After attaining this love, the disciple learns to look at everything from a new perspective and says, "Now, I do not want solutions to my problems, but I need a new perspective because when one looks at things from the perspective of wisdom, all solutions converge into the same approach and all problems are resolved."

In this way, the guru first imparts wisdom, which then builds inner strength that enables the body to make spiritual progress. After that, true devotion awakens within the disciple's heart. All the behavioural patterns and inappropriate tendencies of the body are dissolved in true devotion.

As you start attaining wisdom from the guru, you need to learn something new every day. At the end of the day, if you think that you have not learnt anything new, then the day has been wasted in mundane affairs. The guru's wisdom enjoins the disciple to learn every day, to learn from every mistake, to venture into new activities and learn from new mistakes. If you haven't learned anything new, it implies that you are not disciplined. The disciple, who practices self-discipline, learns something new every day, consciously takes up intentions and gradually gains mastery over his mind and body. He showers his body with true love by giving proper diet and exercises. He makes it his friend through which he can express his benevolent qualities.

❑

10
Testing Time for Narendra

In a conflict between the heart and the brain,
follow your heart.

One day, Narendra's father was returning home after finishing his work in the court. Suddenly, on the way, he started feeling exhausted. Soon after reaching home, he complained of chest pain. Seeing this, Narendra's mother, Bhuvaneshwari Devi, prepared an ointment and applied it on his father's chest which gave him some relief. However, the pain recurred after some time, and he called out to his wife for help. But before she could reach him, Vishwanath Dutt collapsed on the floor. He breathed his last even before the doctor was called for. Unaware of this incident, Narendra was peacefully sleeping at his friend's place after completing his studies.

Narendra's neighbour, Hemali, reached the friend's place late at night and conveyed the news to Narendra in a trembling voice, "Narendra, let's go back home immediately. Everybody is waiting for you. Your father has breathed his last." Narendra was dumbfounded. He could not believe his ears. He had never had to put up with such a tragedy before. It was the saddest incident in his life.

Swami Vivekananda considered two incidents to be the saddest in his life. The first was his father's demise, and the second being the lukewarm response of audiences to his lectures after the initial zeal. After delivering lectures at many places, he observed that it was not bringing about much change in the mindset of the people. After returning from his lectures, he was troubled and sad to learn that the audiences whom he had addressed, had got back to their old ways. People would initially accept the revolutionary perspectives that he delivered to them due to a spark of inspiration but later revert to their old ways and values.

Narendra was deeply grieved by his father's death because he used to consider death to be the gravest agony of all at that time. Later on in his life, Narendra went through immense suffering and hardships, but by then he was well equipped with higher wisdom. He underwent many difficulties after his father's death as his father had not left behind any savings for the family.

Narendra's mother was a pious lady. At that time, when their monthly expenditure used to be one thousand rupees, she reduced the expenditure to merely thirty rupees per month with her thoughtfulness and diligence.

Now, the responsibility of the entire house rested on Narendra's shoulders. As he was not able to earn his living, he found it difficult to make both ends meet. Many of his friends refused to help him, and some of them were afraid to help, thinking that it would hurt Narendra's self-esteem. Being aware of his nature, they were hesitant to offer him any help openly. Sometimes, they would indirectly invite him to a party at their house, but he would decline their invitation thinking how he could enjoy the party when his family members were starving. On days when there was very little or no food at home, he would go out under the pretext that one of his friends had invited him for food, so he would not have food at home. He used to wander in search of a job on an empty stomach.

One morning, while Narendra was busy chanting his prayers while worshipping God, his mother rebuked him, "What can we gain with all this worship? What has God given us? Just give up all this." His mother's words gave a jolt to Narendra. He also began questioning the use of worshipping God so religiously.

Despite several attempts, Narendra could not get a job anywhere. He was somehow passing his days, and his anxiety was rising with every passing day. Gradually, his faith in God started diminishing, and he started moving towards atheism. In the meantime, he also did not get a chance to visit Ramakrishna Paramhansa at Dakshineshwar. Only time would tell whether nature was stringently testing Narendra or whether it was giving him an austere training to prepare him for times to come.

❑

11
The Moral Strength of Narendra's Character

Please everyone without becoming a hypocrite or a coward. When you remain steadfast in your ideal with purity and strength regardless of the obstacles that come your way, the world will follow you in due course.

The life of Vivekananda shows how one can develop a strong character and influence the lives of others. The incidents of his life teach us how we can keep our character pure and resolute despite all kinds of adversities. Let us now look at the incidents from his life.

***

After his father's death, Narendra faced a lot of difficulties in earning a livelihood. Some of his friends had taken to unfair means to earn more. They also offered Narendra to partner with them. At the same time, a rich lady made an indecent proposal to Narendra and in lieu, promised to take care of his financial problems. However, Narendra rejected all these immoral proposals outright.

One of Narendra's friends, who owned a printing press, wanted to earn easy money. Seeing Narendra's financial problems, he proposed that Narendra can write some books. He took Narendra to his house and showed him pornographic books.

Narendra's friend said, "Narendra! These books can help add spice to your writing. Write something that can arouse lust by the mere reading of a word or two, among both men and women alike. We can arrange for the relevant pictures on our own."

Narendra saw those books and immediately threw them on the floor. He thundered with rage, "I will not write any such illicit books, nor will I resort to any unfair and immoral means."

After that, his friend put forward another proposal to translate books written by foreign authors in Bengali and publish them in his name. Narendra rejected that proposal, saying that he would not do anything unrighteous.

His friend's behaviour deeply hurt Narendra, but he continued to conduct himself according to his nature. He did not agree to do any inappropriate work that would blot his character and spoil his family's name.

***

After that, Narendra went to another friend to find some work. This friend was an alcoholic. Worried and dejected, Narendra narrated his tale of misery to his friend. However, this friend considered money as the most important truth of life and God as imagination. However, for Narendra, God was not imagination, rather a state that was difficult, but not impossible to attain.

When Narendra met this friend, he was drinking alcohol. He made several attempts to lure Narendra into drinking but couldn't succeed. He tried hard to convince Narendra in many different ways. However, Narendra strongly resented and said, "Anything that deludes the brain is poison for both the body and the mind, and I will not drink poison."

Both these incidents exhibit Narendra's strength of character. Despite adverse circumstances in life, Narendra never accepted any inappropriate proposals. He always walked the path of righteousness. The family poverty also exposed one more important aspect of Narendra's character. He had a deep sympathy for the poor and oppressed. According to Ramakrishna, had Narendra been raised in luxury, he would have been a different person. He would have become a politician, an advocate, an orator or a social reformer. However, Narendra devoted his life to the service of humanity. Another incident of his life demonstrates his powerful and influential character.

***

Once Narendra's friend from abroad insisted on meeting Narendra's guru Ramakrishna Paramhansa. He said, "I want to meet that great man who has developed a great personality like you."

When Narendra took his friend to his master, the friend was surprised to see the attire of Ramakrishna Paramhansa. He expressed in bewilderment, "How could this man be your guru? He doesn't even have a sense of clothing."

Narendra politely replied, "Dear friend, perhaps in your country, a tailor performs the task of building a character, but in our country, the character is built through thinking and conduct." Narendra's words had such an immense power that it could transform one's mindset.

***

Another incident reflects his strength of character and his love and loyalty for the wellbeing of people. Representatives of all faiths had gathered in the Parliament of World's Religions held in America. Narendra, who had come to be known as Swami Vivekananda by then, was also present. He realised that the American audience didn't have any respect for a Hindu monk coming from India. They considered him inferior. In such a humiliating situation, any common man would have lost his cool, but Swami Vivekananda didn't. He went to the dais and started his speech with, "Sisters and Brothers of America!" His words cast such a magnificent spell on the audience that they continued to applaud for a very long time.

Swami Vivekananda introduced the world with the rich cultural heritage and refined tradition of India. His speech was so influential that it left the audience spellbound. Swami Vivekananda was allotted only five minutes to speak from the dais. However, he spoke for about twenty minutes and was highly appreciated by one and all. After that, his speech was published in all the local newspapers.

To develop a morally strong character, we should lead our lives based on the understanding that character is our most precious treasure. While carrying out our day to day activities, we ought to conduct ourselves in such a manner that the foundation of our character becomes strong and unshakeable.

After reading all these incidents in Narendra's life, we come to know of his many virtues. It is said that a man is known by his friends. However, in case of Narendra, he had friends from diverse backgrounds, but he was an exception. The company of his friends didn't affect him adversely. He always blossomed like an immaculate lotus that stands apart in the dirt.

Every person should choose higher qualities for building their character and mould them according to their goal. They should always strive to make them an inseparable part of their life. A day will surely come when they can become proficient in these qualities. Their character will shine brightly in the aura of these qualities. The ten primary qualities of a strong character are as follows:

1. Impersonal, selfless feeling for the welfare of society.
2. Become proficient in at least one domain of work and master it.
3. Introspection on one's behaviour and thoughts.
4. Self-control – conquer one's sensual tendencies and keep strict control over them.
5. Practice punctuality – use foresight to complete one's work before time.
6. Follow certain principles and abide by certain values in life to always keep one's vision in sight.

7. Fulfill one's responsibilities and develop the courage to take on new responsibilities.
8. Fulfill promises and commitments.
9. Be ever honest – Never compromise with moral values.
10. Maintain purity of mind – safeguard oneself from ill-feelings for others.

Narendra was bestowed with these qualities and had a morally strong character.

❑

12
The Greatest Demand

Be not afraid of anything. You will do marvellous work. It is fearlessness that brings Heaven even in a moment.

Owing to his pitiable financial condition, when Narendra was steeped in distress, he began to have conflicting thoughts. One midnight, when he was returning home, completely drenched in the rain, he heard his inner voice calling out to him. This voice awakened his power of discernment.

When a person firmly believes that there is someone more powerful than him who can solve all his problems, then he prays with all earnestness. As he sees the fruition of his prayers, the feeling of devotion develops within him. Such a deep-rooted devotion was the foundation of Ramakrishna Paramhansa. He strongly believed that all the problems in Narendra's life would be eventually solved. Narendra did not believe in idol worship, but Ramakrishna Paramhansa was a devotee of Goddess Kali. He used to worship the goddess every day.

When a child visits a temple for the first time with his parents, he does not have devotion. He notices that a lot of people come to the temple, place a handkerchief on their head, smear vermillion on their forehead, pray with folded hands and bow before Him. The child also sees them making offerings to the deity and partaking of the prasad. Even if a person gets a little quantity of prasad at the temple, he is delighted. However, if he gets the same quantity at home, he doesn't feel satisfied.

The child also notices that like other people, his parents also stand before the God's idol with folded hands and accept the prasad. The child questions them about these practices. His parents explain that they are praying to God; through prayer, we can communicate with God and ask for anything that we want. On hearing this, the child wonders, "Everyone talks to the idol in the temple, but when would the idol talk to us?" This thought of his gets transformed into a prayer. In this prayer, he urges, "O God, talk to me!" This urge takes the form of a prayer, which is the seed of devotion.

As the child grows up, his prayers also change. When he sees that whatever he has prayed for has been fulfilled, he develops a strong faith in God in his heart. With this strong faith that whatever we ask from God will surely be granted, a prayer arises from the bottom of his heart, "O God; now I do not want anything lesser than you. Anything lesser than you would not satisfy me, and nothing surpasses you in this world."

The same thing happened with Narendra. Depressed with his financial problems, Narendra for the first time asked for something from Ramakrishna Paramhansa. He urged, "You talk to Goddess Kali all the time. Kindly pray to her on behalf of my family so that our life condition improves." Ramakrishna Paramhansa replied, "I do not ask the goddess for such things. Why don't you do it yourself? Today is Tuesday. Go and ask for whatever you wish." Narendra entered the temple and sat before the idol. After some time, deeply immersed in devotion, he had a divine experience and returned from the temple without asking anything.

The next day, Ramakrishna Paramhansa asked Narendra, "Did you ask for anything?" Narendra replied, "No, I couldn't." Then Ramakrishna Paramhansa said, "That's fine. Go and ask again today."

The next day, Narendra again went to the temple, but it repeated. Narendra noticed that Ramakrishna Paramhansa was insisting upon him to go to the temple again and again as if it would be very late if he does not go to the temple immediately. When he was asked to go to the temple the third time, he still could not ask for anything on behalf of his family. He asked Goddess Kali to grant him devotion and the power of renunciation. He returned from the temple. From his seat, Thakur watched Narendra coming out of the temple. Narendra approached him and said, "Thakur, even today, I could not ask for anything for my mother and brothers. Please bless me that my family can overcome this miserable situation. If you so wish, their needs would be fulfilled."

Thakur replied, "Do you have faith in me?"

Narendra replied, "Yes, I have full faith in you."

Thakur looked at Narendra who was still holding his feet firmly. Then Thakur replied, "Narendra, go home and rest assured. There would never be any scarcity of food and clothing at your house henceforth."

Soon after this incident, Narendra's life began to change. He got a job of a translator. Later he also got a job as a teacher. This ensured an assured income and arrangement of food for him and his family. Although his life was not as luxurious as it used to be, he did not have to wander in search of his livelihood.

He used to visit Ramakrishna Paramhansa once or twice a week. Devotional songs would be sung; music would be played, following which Ramakrishna would revel in the state of Samadhi; after emerging out of that state, he would share his divine experiences. Narendra was able to comprehend only a part of what Ramakrishna Paramhansa spoke. However, Ramakrishna Paramhansa always loved Narendra dearly. He always praised him and forgave his mistakes. However, Narendra continued to have doubts about his master.

❑

13
Narendra becomes a True Disciple

The greatest religion is to be true to your own nature. Have faith in yourself.

Narendra was an honest disciple and his master Ramakrishna Paramhansa was a straightforward guru. At a very young age, Narendra had the maturity of an advanced disciple, while Ramakrishna Paramhansa was a guru with a childlike curiosity and emotions at his ripe age. Owing to his maturity and physical built, Narendra looked like a youth of twenty years, merely at the young age of sixteen.

In this master-disciple pair, the disciple was honest, and the guru was equally unpretentious. Vivekananda always put across his views to people with utmost sincerity and never deceived his guru. In modern times, however, it is common for people to resort to deceit for the sake of name, fame, position and other gains.

Ramakrishna Paramhansa never saw Narendra as a mere physical body, but rather as an embodiment of God. From the very beginning, he had identified Narendra's virtues and noticed his simplicity and honesty.

In case certain things influence you negatively or the sermons of your master have a negative effect on you due to the preconceived notions of your mind, then it is important to inform your master about it. However, dishonest people tend to keep certain things secretive, they do not disclose them to anybody, and drift away from the path of Truth by making wrong assumptions. When the disciple confides in his guru that a certain teaching hurts him, the guru can then explain how the teaching was not meant to lead to such a result. If the disciple is getting a different result, then it only means that he has not understood the point from its right perspective. After that, the master can explain the correct meaning of the teaching to his disciple. Once the disciple can understand the meaning correctly, he would start experiencing the positive effect immediately. Therefore, it is the responsibility of every disciple to disclose everything to his master. Narendra also used to convey everything to his guru without any deceit.

Narendra often told his master, "When you say that you can see Goddess Kali, I think there is something wrong with your mind. It is a mere hallucination." By saying such things, Narendra used to doubt Ramakrishna Paramhansa's experience, but Ramakrishna never considered it to be offensive. Instead, he would reply, "Oh! Is that so? I would get it clarified from Mother Kali!" He would then go to the temple and smilingly return and reply, "It is not so. Mother says that Narendra is very young now. He would not understand this until he grows up."

Ramakrishna Paramhansa had such an immense faith in Narendra that whenever an intellectual came to meet him, he would get Narendra to strike a conversation with that person on a specific topic in his presence. During the discussion, he would take delight in the way Narendra would participate in the discussion and say, "What a nice explanation!" Narendra couldn't comprehend why his master was behaving this way. Later, he realised that it was just a divine play of his master. Narendra would muse over how effectively he had handled the conversation, how he had logically put across his points to the intellectual, also quoting references from several books.

Ramakrishna Paramhansa would only listen to what Narendra used to say.

On several occasions, Narendra also tested his guru. He knew that Ramakrishna Paramhansa never touched money. Therefore, once he placed a coin under his master's pillow. As soon as Ramakrishna came and sat on the bed, he immediately got up and started looking around. Seeing the master perturbed, one of his disciples asked him what happened. Ramakrishna replied that he was getting strange vibes from the bed and asked the disciple to check it out. When the disciple removed the bedsheet, the coin fell on the floor. Ramakrishna looked at Narendra and at once understood that it was Narendra who had played the mischief. Narendra quickly slipped away from the scene.

Narendra would often experiment and check whether Ramakrishna Paramhansa was an evolved soul or he had some mental disorder. He wanted to check whether he saw Goddess Kali or it was an extension of his imagination.

An immature disciple often has doubts in his mind. Narendra was unable to understand the love and affection Ramakrishna had for him. Therefore he used to tell him, "You would also meet the same fate as King Bharata. The king had developed a deep affection for his deer at the time of his death. He had to take the form of a deer in his subsequent life, because of which he could not attain salvation. You also love me so dearly. This attachment would create bondage, and you may not be able to liberate yourself." To this Ramakrishna would reply, "Is that so? I would immediately go and ask Mother Kali." He would then say, "What you are saying is right. Your logic seems right to me. But what can I do? I do not find peace unless I see you." After that, he would go to the temple, and then after returning, he would reply, "It is not so! The mother told me that since I see you as an embodiment of God, I have developed such deep affection for you. The day I stop seeing God inside you, I would not like to see you again."

Narendra would keep asking questions. He would reflect on the answers received from Ramakrishna as to how they could be right. Narendra's queries and doubts were often related to how God could assume the form of a human being. He was of the opinion that it was the job of the ignorant to imagine about God and make His idols. Owing to such doubts, he was unable to understand Ramakrishna Paramhansa because he was not mature enough to follow what his master said. As time passed and he assessed Ramakrishna Paramhansa from various angles, he gradually started understanding his master.

One day Ramakrishna was sitting inside a room, while Narendra was laughingly discussing something with one of his friends outside. He said, "This pot is Brahman; This bowl is also Brahman." Narendra was making fun of Ramakrishna's statements. Meanwhile, Ramakrishna came out of the room and touched Narendra. Instantly, Narendra got transported into the state of Samadhi. Swami Vivekananda wrote about this experience in his autobiography that after coming back to his house, he remained in that state for two days. The same experience continued while he returned home as well. He felt the presence of God everywhere. When it was time to have his meal, he would keep sitting in front of the food. When his mother used to question him what happened to him, he would feel that the food that was placed in front of him also had God inside and whoever would consume the food also had God inside. Many times, he would be lost and could not remember what to do, when and where. After two days, when he became somewhat normal, he realised that whatever he had read in the religious scriptures and the *Vedas* during past so many years, he was experientially knowing that now. After realizing the state of Samadhi, it took Narendra three years to become a matured disciple.

❑

14
Narendra becomes a Devotee

They alone live, who live for others.

Everything changed when Narendra became a mature disciple. Earlier, Ramakrishna used to wait for him and ask everyone whether Narendra had come. But now it was just the opposite. When Narendra stopped testing his master, Ramakrishna Paramhansa started testing his disciple.

Whenever Narendra used to come and sit near Ramakrishna Paramhansa, he would neither look at him nor ask him to sing. There used to be several activities every day in the ashram, but nobody would pay attention to Narendra. During discussions, everybody gathered and sat near Ramakrishna Paramhansa. There would be question and answer sessions, but nobody would talk to Narendra at all.

One month passed, but Ramakrishna Paramhansa continued to behave in the same manner. Narendra kept visiting him as usual. After another month passed, Ramakrishna asked Narendra, "Narendra! I have not talked to you for the past several days, nor have I looked at you, then why do you still keep coming to me?" Narendra replied, "I do not come here to listen to you. Rather I come to see you." Ramakrishna gathered that Narendra had transformed from being a mere disciple into being a true devotee. He was happy to see that Narendra was now ready to move ahead on his path. However, Ramakrishna tested him further.

Ramakrishna Paramhansa knew the various practices that were prevalent in all the religious faiths in the name of seeking God. He had undertaken all kinds of spiritual practices and had studied the practices being followed in religions like Hinduism, Islam, Sikhism, Christianity, etc.

One day he told Narendra, "I have acquired several occult powers while performing spiritual practices. Now I want to pass on those powers to you." It was a big testing time for Narendra. He was getting the powers for free, which could otherwise have taken long years of penance. It was difficult for Narendra to refuse the offer.

Narendra asked Ramakrishna Paramhansa, "What would I gain by acquiring these powers?" The master replied, "After you attain true wisdom, these powers will help you in expressing your true nature." This put Narendra into a deeper dilemma. It was all the more difficult for him to refuse the offer because he could see that those powers would be useful to him. Then Narendra thought over for a while and again asked, "Would these powers help me realise God?" Ramakrishna Paramhansa replied in negative. Narendra quickly replied, "If it is so, then I do not need these powers. I need first to realise God. I would think about these powers later."

Narendra was such an exemplary disciple who never aspired to anything lesser than Self-realization. He aspired to attain only that for which he had an insatiable uncompromising thirst. Ramakrishna Paramhansa used to tell him, "In whichever form you call upon God and meditate on him, continue to do so. If you want to accept God in the manner you want to, then continue your pursuit. The day your prayer is answered, you will develop faith in that form and follow that." That's why Narendra refused the proposal of occult powers saying that he did not want to get stuck in them and go astray. He didn't want to miss the wood for trees.

Ramakrishna Paramhansa had several disciples. One day he decided to ordain them to Sanyasa (the path of renunciation). He called some of them and told Narendra, "You are their leader. Wear these ochre robes and go out to seek alms. Would you be able to do it?" Narendra replied in affirmative. This was a test to check if Narendra had got the better of his ego.

The guru would want such an exemplary disciple who does not aspire to anything other than God. He only desires to attain the ultimate state of consciousness. Swami Vivekananda was one such remarkable disciple.

❑

15
Freedom from Lust and Greed

Strength is life; Weakness is death.
The expansion is life; Contraction is death.
Love is life; Hatred is death.

Ramakrishna Paramhansa stressed the need for freedom from lust and greed because he knew that these vices deluded many people. Man has complicated the understanding of lust and greed through the perversion of thought. Their real purpose is something altogether different.

Nature designs every species to sustain, survive and procreate. Procreation helps the species to continue its existence, to evolve. In the process, the development of nature is continued. To fulfil this objective, the feeling and process of sex came into being. However, man has taken this feeling into its other extreme and distorted the feeling of sex, thereby perverting it into what is called lust. Let us understand this with the help of an example.

We all know the objective of food – it is to provide the essential nutrients and energy to the body to keep the body healthy. However, today, very few people are taking food with this sole objective. People eat to cater to their taste buds and satisfy their cravings. If the food is delicious and as per one's liking, then one eats it even when it is not required and eats more than what is required. After overeating, they take help of digestive medicines to digest the food, to be able to eat again. In this way, a normal act, which was aimed towards providing good health to the body, has now become the reason for the disease of the body.

This is how a natural activity has been perverted into a harmful tendency and a medium of entertainment for people. It has led to dissatisfaction and disease.

The fault does not lie in the act of eating, but in the way one thinks about food. The same thing applies to sex as well. By social norms, it is normal to have loving and harmonious sexual relationship between husband and wife while maintaining the dignity of marriage, which gives birth to a new healthy generation. However, when exploitation creeps in here or when it is made into a tool for enjoyment, it leads to corruption of values and mental affliction. At the end of this, all thoughts tend to revolve around this aspect of life; people get into premarital or extramarital relations, thereby converting what was a sacred mechanism of nature into lust and disease; this becomes the cause for the downfall of humanity. This becomes extremely damaging to the person, his family and society as a whole.

Ramakrishna Paramhansa also guided disciples on this aspect because he knew that once lust overpowers man's reasoning, it kills his conscience and causes him to indulge indiscriminately in thoughts and feelings of lust, becoming a serious disease that leads to various psychological and physical problems. It gives rise to immorality. As a result, families get disintegrated, and lives of several people are ruined. Lust also gives rise to serious offences in the society and therefore, everybody, especially the youth should be aware of the dangers of lust.

During the days of his youth, Narendra always obeyed his guru. He tried to implement all his teachings. Ramakrishna Paramhansa had full faith in Narendra that he would never indulge in activities of lust. One of the incidents of his life demonstrates how he implemented the teachings of his master and obeyed his directives.

Some of Ramakrishna's disciples were upset with the special importance that Narendra was getting from his master. They often complained about Narendra to Ramakrishna Paramhansa saying, "Narendra has got into wrong company. His friends consume alcohol and also visit prostitutes for immoral activities." During those days, a prostitute named Kantimohini had become popular in Kolkata.

Once, Narendra's friends wanted to test whether Narendra was pious and sattvic or whether Ramakrishna was praising him for no reason. They took Narendra to Kantimohini on a false pretext. Narendra was told that an acquaintance invited them for meals. After reaching the place, Narendra began to feel a bit uncomfortable, so he took rest for a while. When he opened his eyes, he found himself alone in the house; all his friends had left.

As he was about to leave the house, Kantimohini arrived. Narendra was astonished to see her. He politely requested her to allow him to go, but she did not pay heed to him. She tried to entice Narendra with her flirtatious gestures and words but did not succeed. When she saw that all her efforts are going in vain, she fell at Narendra's feet and requested him to forgive her.

Listening to her, Narendra's voice became stern. He had never seen a woman in such a form. He considered every woman as his mother. He retorted to her, "Stop! To please this earthly body, you may have committed immoral activities so far. Have you ever tried to go beyond life and death? Give up your low intellect and seek the shelter of God. He would surely help you. Also, stop this hypocrisy, lest no man would ever trust any good-natured, poor woman."

Kantimohini was stunned with Narendra's words. She had not met such an upright man before.

Narendra's friends were watching all this from behind the window. They were dumbfounded with his remarks. They realised their mistake and were convinced that Narendra was indeed an earnest seeker of Truth, free from all attachments of lust and greed, who could not be entrapped in any worldly bondage.

During the last days of Ramakrishna Paramhansa, Narendra called all his brother disciples, lit a ceremonial fire and said, "Like a true monk, now we will bring out and surrender our hidden attachments for lust and greed and oblate them in this ceremonial fire to purify our hearts. In this pure blazing fire, not only lust, but all our desires shall be reduced to ashes." Everybody got transported into a divinely ecstatic state. They felt that all their earthly desires were indeed burning to ashes, their minds were becoming purer and advanced to possess sattvic qualities at a fast pace. Whatever worldly matter the mind was filled with was being emptied and was being filled with divinity. In this way, Narendra freed everybody from the attachments of lust and greed.

The close disciples of Ramakrishna Paramhansa could renounce their desires for lust at the level of thought itself. They had the clarity and understanding of their role in this world. They clearly knew that their bodies were not meant for begetting children but to attain salvation and raise mass consciousness.

Let's not misunderstand here that the role of a monk is superior to that of a householder who gives birth to children. This certainly does not mean that a noble householder who rears a family is bad or inferior. It does not help to judge any role within the limits of good and bad. Every role has its importance in nature. Had Vishwanath Dutt and Bhuvaneshwari Devi not given birth to Swami Vivekananda, such a remarkable luminary would have never graced the world!

We need to avoid both the extremes and follow the middle path. In the middle, there is the path of the Bright Householder which transcends the ways of both, the recluse and the householder. A Bright householder very clearly knows that he is not the body, that he is rather a form of Rama, the Self, which governs the body. When he is fixed on this Truth, no lust or worldly desire entangles him. In fact, lust or any other desire can entrap us only when we drift away from our true essence – the immaculate Self. Contrary to this, when we are centred on the Truth, unselfish desires arise in our heart which is meant for the expression of Truth and a selfless life.

❑

16

Narendra, the Ascetic

Anything that makes weak – physically, intellectually and spiritually, reject it as poison.

Imagine that there is a village. Whoever enters the village cannot know from which corner an arrow or spear would come and pierce him, from which corner a stone would be hurled at him, or when someone could suddenly throw dust in his eyes.

Suppose you have to visit that village for some important work. How would you go there? Every person who wishes to enter the village is first interviewed. The interview is taken by a person sitting at the village gate, and he has the authority to decide whether you are fit to enter the village or not.

The interviewer, who also happens to be a trainer, knows what happens in the village. So, he ascertains beforehand whether the visitor would be able to go through the village safely or whether he would be wounded. He knows that if the person gets injured, he would be in bad condition, his clothes would be torn and he would bleed. Therefore, he feels that it is better to examine and assess a person before he enters the village. The interview plays an important role as a prerequisite for entering this village.

Before entering this village, you need to get trained in meditation because you have very little knowledge about this place. If your focus is not trained, then you will not be able to spot an arrow that is suddenly shot at you. The practice of meditation teaches you what you should do before the arrow hits you.

Essentially, you need to raise your level of awareness first. When an arrow is shot, it makes a distinct sound. You need to train your focus to locate that sound. If you are not properly trained, you will miss the sound, and the arrow is bound to pierce you. Later, you may repent, it would have been better, had you been more aware and alert.

This story of the village is an analogy. This village is nothing but the illusory world that we live in. If you are not aware and alert in this world, then the arrows of illusion will pierce you. This means that negative thoughts and tendencies can entrap and hurt you, worsening the state of your mind. Therefore, it is important to get trained in meditation first before entering the illusory world.

Meditation raises your level of awareness and sensitivity. There are many such arrows in the illusory world, which can hurt the person internally. One needs to undergo the training of meditation to safeguard oneself from these arrows. Swami Vivekananda also used to meditate every day. An incident from his life particularly reveals how deeply he used to meditate and to what extent he used to be absorbed in it.

Narendra used to visit Dakshineshwar every day and discuss with Ramakrishna. He used to meditate as per his master's guidelines. Ramakrishna Paramhansa was very pleased with his spiritual practice.

One day, another disciple named Girish also accompanied Narendra to Dakshineshwar. Girish also sat for meditation along with Narendra, but he was unable to concentrate his mind. He experienced biting sensations at various points on his body. Despite these disturbing sensations, he did not open his eyes but gently slapped on those points of the body. Probably, he was being bitten by some mosquitoes. Had it been a few mosquitoes, it would have still been fine, but it appeared that there were dozens of mosquitoes. Girish could either focus on meditation or get rid of the mosquitoes. Even if his focus was on the stillness of the meditative state, when the mosquitoes tortured his body severely, his focus drifted to the painful sensations.

When Girish was about to open his eyes, he was suddenly reminded of Narendra. He thought if Narendra had opened his eyes, he would have surely made some arrangement to get rid of the mosquitoes. But he did not hear anything from Narendra. It implied that Narendra was meditating despite these perturbing mosquito bites. He considered that if Narendra had not accepted defeat from the mosquitoes then why should he.

He did not want to be defeated alongside Narendra. But the fact was that he was being bitten by the mosquitoes so severely that it was becoming difficult for him to restrain himself from hitting them. The mosquitoes had ruthlessly bitten him all over the body. Given a chance, he would have mercilessly hit them.

After a while, Girish again considered, "How can I assume that Narendra is still seated quietly in meditation, just because he has not yet called anyone for help? Possibly he has opened his eyes long ago and might be watching me in distress. Maybe, he is enjoying the sight of me being bitten by the mosquitoes. It is also possible that he has tiptoed back to the temple so that after I get troubled searching for him here and there, he could laugh at me."

The fact, however, was that all these were mere figments of his imagination. Finally, Girish became impatient and opened his eyes. He saw that Narendra was seated unperturbed at his place, with eyes closed. He was deeply absorbed in meditation. Girish was flabbergasted to see Narendra in that state. In the light of the sacred fire burning nearby, he noticed that it wasn't one or two, but countless mosquitoes on Narendra's body.

Watching Narendra immersed in deep meditation, Girish felt ashamed about how his intellect had entertained such baseless thoughts. His ego was shattered. He realised that only an earnest seeker of Truth could be absorbed in meditation the way Narendra was.

❑

17
The Importance of the Guru in Narendra's Life

Purity, patience and perseverance are the three essentials to success and, above all, love.

Narendra had an unparalleled devotion to his guru. He dedicated his entire life to the service of his guru Ramakrishna Paramhansa. During his last days on earth, Ramakrishna Paramhansa had fallen extremely ill. Narendra used to be in the service of his guru during the entire day. He used to take full care of his guru's chores without being bothered about his own family or food. He was thoroughly involved in the service of his guru with complete attention and dedication. The following incident from that period provides a glimpse of his devotion towards his guru.

Ramakrishna Paramhansa's health was deteriorating day by day. All the disciples were serving him in turns. Narendra used to stay with him almost twenty-four hours a day. One day, he asked the other brother disciples to take care of Thakur, and he went out for some work. When he returned, he saw all of them sitting in the courtyard looking at each other. They were all looking extremely worried. Narendra could not understand the cause of their concern. When he approached them, he saw no sign of enthusiasm on their faces, nor was anyone eager to share what had happened in his absence.

They were all sitting quietly. Nobody was able to muster enough courage to tell Narendra about Thakur's health. Narendra looked at each of their faces by turn and understood that they were certainly hiding something from him.

At last, after being repeatedly asked by Narendra, one of them said, "Doctor had visited to see Thakur. He said that Thakur is suffering from a contagious disease, and anybody serving him might also get infected by the disease. Therefore, we all have been asked to be careful."

Narendra understood their concern. Of all the disciples of Ramakrishna, he was the most mature one. He was able to witness the divine play of God. He asked everyone to accompany him into their master's room.

Narendra did not have any doubt or dilemma in his mind. Unhesitatingly, he started proceeding towards Thakur's room. All the other disciples also followed him.

The door of Thakur's room was open. Thakur was taking an afternoon nap. A disciple was sitting near him. Narendra gestured him to come out. The disciple tiptoed out of the room.

Narendra asked him, "Has Thakur taken his lunch?"

The disciple replied, "Mother Sarada had given him a very salty soft porridge thinking that if Thakur is unable to swallow it, at least he could sip it easily. However, he was unable to consume even that. So, he ate very little from his plate. While eating his food, he had a bout of cough due to which he could not eat further and left the rest of the food on the plate."

Narendra went into the room, picked up the plate and came out. He touched the plate with his lips and quickly drank the remaining porridge in a single gulp. All the disciples were shocked to see this.

Narendra told them, "Henceforth, none of us would discuss the contagiousness of Thakur's disease."

This incident reflects the true devotion of Swami Vivekananda towards his guru. He always accorded the highest importance to the instructions of his guru and propagated his divine teachings to the entire world. In this way, he established an example of ultimate devotion and loyalty towards his guru.

While guiding his brother disciples he used to say, "Exactly as a child needs his mother, so does the disciple need a guru. Without the guru, life is not meaningless, but it is less meaningful. People, who do not have a guru in their life, settle for a very shallow level of happiness. The presence of a true guru is paramount for those who want to explore the highest possibilities in their lives. Blessed are we, who have got the guru like Thakur."

As soon as we understand the role of the guru in our lives, his grace begins to shower upon us. It is indeed the guru who helps us to reach this state of receptivity to his grace. He instructs us to perform certain experiments through listening to the Truth, contemplation upon the Truth, reading of books related to Truth and service unto the Truth. A disciple always stands to benefit when he abides by the instructions of the guru without any doubts. The effect of Truth in his life begins to become more evident. When a disciple recognises the real essence of his guru in entirety, for the first time he experiences true joy, love and devotion in his life. He derives immense happiness in the service of his guru. The guru engages the disciple in service so that the remnants of his ego also get shattered. Therefore, the disciple should continue serving his guru in all possible ways. If the service is rendered in the right spirit with correct understanding, it can lead to Self-realization.

Falling in love with the guru is like falling in love with God. It is the doorway to the attainment of the ultimate purpose of human life. It is essential to understand the importance of the guru as the most important presence in our life. A true seeker of Truth should remain in the company of his guru every day, at least mentally, if not physically.

❑

18
Living Disciple and Formless Master

The powers of the mind are like the rays of the sun; when they are concentrated, they illumine.

In the course of life's journey, Ramakrishna Paramhansa was gradually transcending the realm of physical form. His condition worsened in August 1886. Once, when he felt a bit relieved from his ailment at midnight, he called Narendra by his side and delivered his last instruction in the presence of all the other disciples, "Now, I will not stay with you for long. But even after I leave this mortal body, I want you all to remain together. I know that it is not possible for people of the same age group to live together in such a large number as they often have differences of opinion. Therefore, I enjoin you that you all must obey what Narendra says and abide by his instructions. You must never abandon him at any cost, under any circumstances. Do any of you have any objection to this?"

Thakur's instruction was not such that anybody would object to it. After all, all the disciples used to hold Narendra in high regard, and his wish was a command for them.

Thakur looked at Narendra and said, "I'm leaving all my sons in your custody. Please take care of them. It should not happen that after I pass away, they give up their spiritual practice and return to their old ways with their respective families. It is your responsibility to see that they continue their spiritual pursuit."

For Narendra, obeying his master's command was like worshipping God. He assured Ramakrishna Paramhansa that he would always abide by his instructions. Thakur's throat pain was aggravating. He was unable to talk any further and remained in silence for a long time. All the disciples also sat in meditation. After a while, when Narendra opened his eyes, he saw that Thakur was crying.

Thakur hid neither his tears nor his emotions. When Narendra enquired, he replied, "Today I have handed over everything to you. The Mother Goddess who used to reside in this body will henceforth reside in your body. After giving you everything, I have now come to nought."

Narendra was speechless. He simply looked at his guru with utter reverence. He asked everyone to recite "Hari Om Tat Sat". At the same time, they also sang a devotional hymn. At midnight, Ramakrishna Paramhansa loudly uttered the name of his dearest mother Goddess Kali three times and then being absorbed in the state of Samadhi, he cast off his mortal body.

Now, the disciple had a mortal body while the guru had transcended his physical body. He had become formless. It was as if Ramakrishna Paramhansa was experiencing himself and enacting through the body of his disciple Swami Vivekananda. All these truths are beyond logical reasoning, hence cannot be explained rationally.

Between Swami Vivekananda and Ramakrishna Paramhansa, the disciple had a form and the guru was formless. Just before leaving his body, the guru had initiated the disciple and made him experience Samadhi. After being initiated by the guru, Swami Vivekananda commenced his mission. Swami Vivekananda lived with his master for five years. During this time, he received profound wisdom from him, understood the crux of Vedanta and learned to abide by the experience of the Self. Later on, he promoted and propagated all these teachings throughout the world.

The holy mortal remains of Ramakrishna Paramhansa were consigned to flames in the cremation ground on the banks of the Ganga. When Sarada Devi began to adopt certain external ways befitting a Hindu widow, she heard Thakur's assurance from within, "I have not died. I have just moved from one room to another."

After returning from the crematorium, the disciples had an overwhelming feeling of emptiness. Ramakrishna Paramhansa was more than a father figure to them. Now his sermons and his memories were the source of inspiration for them. They could still hear his words echoing in their ears. However, they could not see him physically, nor enjoy his divine smile.

A week after Ramakrishna Paramhansa had left his mortal body, one night, Narendra was taking a stroll with his fellow disciple in a garden. Suddenly, he saw a divine figure in front of him. Undoubtedly, it was Ramakrishna Paramhansa. Assuming that it was his hallucination, Narendra kept quiet and stood still at his place. However, his fellow disciple exclaimed in surprise, "Narendra, Look! Look!" Now there wasn't an iota of doubt. Narendra was convinced that it was Ramakrishna Paramhansa himself, who had appeared in that divine form. When he called out to his other fellow disciples to have a glimpse of Thakur, the figure disappeared. Narendra realised that it so happened because the Guru is not a mere physical body. In fact, the Guru is the Consciousness that resides in all of us and in which we all reside. When this Consciousness reveals itself completely, then it is known as Self-realization. The same Consciousness guides us along our spiritual journey.

Narendra understood the divine play of God – till then Consciousness had been guiding them in the form of Ramakrishna

Paramhansa. Though his body was no more amidst them, the Consciousness was still present. Henceforth, through whichever form the Consciousness would guide them, they ought to remain receptive to it.

❑

PART – 3

Expression of Discernment and Devotion

19

A Journey around India – The beginning of Swami Vivekananda's Expression

Desire, ignorance and inequality –
This is the trinity of bondage.

The young disciples of Ramakrishna Paramhansa, who were inspired by him and were desirous of leading an ascetic life, needed a place where they could live together as a group of renunciates. Narendra was eager to bring the renunciate disciples together so that they could live and function as a group with a mission. However, the question was who would bear the expenses of the house where these youth would stay, how would their food and necessities of life be fulfilled. However, in some days, all this got arranged.

By the generosity of a close follower of Ramakrishna Paramhansa, all these problems were sorted out. He took over the responsibility of providing shelter to these young disciples of Thakur upon himself. With his help, a house was taken on lease in Baranagar, situated between Kolkata and Dakshineshwar. Being dilapidated and desolate, that house was infamous as a haunted house. However, given that the house was away from the hustle and bustle of Kolkata city, the young disciples were very happy to stay in that deserted house. This place came to be known as Baranagar Math, which was the first centre of the monks of Ramakrishna Order.

The disciples built a small temple commemorating Thakur in the house, where Thakur's cot was placed. They used to prepare the bed, offer meals and conduct worship every day in this temple. After that, they also used to meditate in that temple.

Now, Narendra devoted himself with all his heart and soul in training his fellow disciples. During daytime, he would go home and attend to his domestic responsibilities and then return to the Math in the evening. They all would practice evening meditation together. Narendra's presence was a source of joy and inspiration for everybody.

After some days, one of the fellow disciple's mother invited them to a village called Antpur. So, they took a break from their stringent spiritual routine at Baranagar. Narendra initiated everyone into monk-hood and designated them with their spiritual names. On his way to America in 1893, Narendra permanently adopted the name "Swami Vivekananda" for himself. Before this, he used names like "Vividishananda" and "Sachidananda" to maintain the secrecy of his identity. The names of other fellow disciples were as follows –

Rakhaal Chandra Ghosh	Swami Brahmananda
Jogindranath Chowdhury	Swami Yogananda
Nitya Niranjan Ghosh	Swami Niranjanananda
Latu	Swami Adbhutananda
Baburam Ghosh	Swami Premananda
Tarak Nath Ghosal	Swami Shivananda
Harinath Chattopadhyay	Swami Turiyananda
Sarat Chandra Chakravarty	Swami Sardananda
Sashi Bhusan Chakravarty	Swami Ramkrishnananda
Kali Prasad Chandra	Swami Abhedananda
Gangadhar Ghatak	Swami Akhandananda
Gopal Chandra Ghosh (elder)	Swami Advaitananda

Sarada Prasanna Mitra	Swami Trigunatitananda
Subodh Chandra Ghosh	Swami Subodhananda
Hari Prasanna Chaterjee	Swami Vijnanananda
Tulasi Charan Dutta	Swami Nirmalananda

After returning to Baranagar, all these youth relinquished their house and became permanent residents of the Math. They started leading an arduous life of an ascetic. Such a life of hardships played a vital role in their spiritual practice. However, some householder disciples of Thakur did not take a liking to their penance. One of them would repeatedly ask with sarcasm, "By merely renouncing worldly affairs, have you attained God!?" Narendra would give a sharp reply, "Even if we don't attain God as you say, does it mean that we should give up our spiritual practice leading to a higher way of life at the cost of adopting a life driven by sensory attractions?"

The young monks of Baranagar Math sought to experience complete surrender, renunciation and inner peace through a nomadic lifestyle of a renunciate. They aspired to enrich their spiritual life all the more by visiting places of pilgrimage.

Narendra was now desirous to examine his inner strength by leading a life of solitude. At the same time, he also wanted his fellow disciples to become independent. Before he commenced the life of a mendicant, some of his fellow disciples had already left on pilgrimages. Initially, Narendra took up a couple of small sojourns, after which he would return to Baranagar. However, in 1890, he abandoned everything and set out on a pilgrimage to India. This time, he was lost in the sheer expanse of his motherland. In 1893, when his fellow disciples managed to trace his whereabouts, he had already gained fame as "Swami Vivekananda" in the city of Chicago in America.

As part of his pilgrimage to India, Narendra first visited Varanasi – the holy city blessed with the presence of many monks and saints. Narendra visited temples and met sages and saints.

While staying on the banks of the holy Ganga, he also met Trailang Swami, who was immersed in a deep meditative state.

One day, some monkeys started chasing after Narendra in Varanasi. He started running to get rid of them. Suddenly, another mendicant shouted at him, "Stop! Don't run away from them. Face them courageously." Narendra stopped and stared at the monkeys without fear. Looking at his fearless stance, all the monkeys immediately fled the spot. Swami Vivekananda would refer to this incident on many occasions in his lectures later and urge his audience to face problems courageously instead of running away from them.

Everybody in this world has been given a different set of problems. People are entrusted with problems to build their capabilities so as to enable them to play a certain role in the future. If you are told about your future role in this world today, you won't get stressed about it.

Take the example of Helen Keller. She was deaf, dumb and blind by birth. How could such a physically challenged girl acquire an education? Despite her shortcomings, Helen Keller grew up and authored many books. Even today, she is cited as the epitome of courage and determination in the schools for the blind. The students are told that if Helen Keller could do it, so can they. She has become an inspiration for the blind. How did this happen? In those days being blind, dumb and deaf was a formidable problem for Helen Keller, but now it is evident that her problems had emerged as a challenge to solve the problems of others like her.

If you look at your problem with this understanding, you would be surprised that the problem is not at all yours. You have been given the problem so that others can benefit from your experience and get solutions to their problems.

Once while travelling in Rajputana, Swami Vivekananda engaged in continuous discussions on spirituality for three nights and three days. Nobody paid heed to his meals or rest. After everybody had left, a lower caste man approached him with much hesitation. He served him some raw food. He was considered an untouchable as per the orthodox caste system prevalent then and was prohibited from offering cooked food. However, Swami Vivekananda did not believe in caste discrimination. He gladly accepted the food. After having his meal, when Swami Vivekananda expressed his gratitude, the man felt overwhelmed and shed tears of delight. Seeing him emotionally overwhelmed, Swami Vivekananda mulled about the welfare of thousands of such noble souls who lived in abject poverty and who were castigated as untouchables.

There are countless such incidents from Swami Vivekananda's life which serve as an inspiration to follow the path of Truth.

❑

20

Swami Vivekananda demystifies the Secret of Idol Worship

The greatest sin is to think yourself weak.

Should one worship idols or not? What is the objective of idol worship? Such questions arise in the minds of many, but very few find the right answers and unearth the secret behind idol worship. When you sit in front of an idol and reflect over the deity's qualities and meditate, a vibration originates from it which awakens your inner being. You then experience the presence of God in that idol itself. If you can experience God in the idol made of stone, you can certainly experience the existence of the Almighty inside living human beings! Those who have realised this secret started idol-worship with the understanding that people can realise the ultimate Truth even in an idol made of stone.

While journeying through different parts of India, Swami Vivekananda imparted this understanding to King Mangal Singh of Alwar. One day he was camping in the city of Alwar in Rajasthan. King Mangal Singh was considered as an egoistic ruler. The king's chief minister was a great devotee of Swamiji. Swami Vivekananda never used to stay at any place for too long. Therefore, the minister urged the king that he should try and meet Swami Vivekananda at least once, as it was not certain whether he would ever get a chance to meet such an exalted monk again.

King Mangal Singh could have easily invited Swami Vivekananda to his palace, but he didn't. He wanted to ascertain whether Swamiji was worthy of being his guest. Therefore, he went to meet Swami Vivekananda and challenged him with questions on his survival by begging alms. In response, Swamiji gave fitting replies and also pointed out the king's shortcomings. He also gave him a cue on how a king ought to discharge his duties towards his subjects.

King Mangal Singh felt ashamed upon hearing Swamiji's words. When he realised his mistake, he surrendered himself at his feet and invited Swamiji to his palace, so that he could suitably honour him. Swamiji knew that King Mangal Singh did not believe in idol worship. Therefore, he visited his palace and demystified the secret behind idol worship.

When Swamiji reached the palace, King Mangal Singh welcomed him with due respect and loyalty. The king knelt before Swamiji and apologised, "Please forgive me Swamiji as I could not recognise you earlier." Raising him to his throne, Swamiji assured, "Repentance cleanses one of all committed sins. If you still have any guilt left in your heart, let go of it and make your mind completely unblemished. Engage your mind in the devotion of the Lord."

Mangal Singh somberly replied, "But I don't believe in idol worship. I have no faith in a God made of metal, paper or clay. So, what is the point in nurturing devotion to the Lord? Would I be punished for this too after my death?" Swamiji benevolently replied, "Why would you be punished for it? You can carry on with worship according to your belief, and you would not be punished at all." Everybody was surprised by Swamiji's reply because he used to visit temples himself and worship God in the form of deities. And here he was, assuring the king that the king would not be punished if he did not worship God. People assumed that Swamiji might have been frightened of the king, due to which he was singing the tune of the king.

King Mangal Singh raised another question before Swamiji, "Do you mean to say that one should not indulge in idol worship?" At this, Swamiji smilingly looked at a picture of the king hanging on the wall and urged, "Please take off this picture from the wall." Accordingly, the picture was removed from the wall and brought in front of Swamiji. As per his instructions, the picture was placed flat on the floor. Swamiji then asked the minister, "Please spit on this picture. Anybody is welcome to spit on it. Is it of any significance? It is nothing but a mere picture. Does anyone have any objection to spitting on it?"

The minister was completely bemused. At last, he somehow overcame his restraint and exclaimed, "What are you saying Swamiji? This resembles our king. How can I insult it?"

Swamiji replied, "What's the harm in doing so? The king is not physically present in this picture. It is a mere canvas. It neither speaks like the king nor can it move or behave like the king. And still, you are refusing to spit on it. Why? It is because you find the glimpse of your king in this piece of paper. Therefore, you consider it as an insult to the king, if someone spits on this painted canvas."

Now Swamiji turned towards the king and said, "O King! Do you see this? Even though you are not physically present in the picture, you are still very much present in it. That is why your loyal minister is so distressed by my words. When he looks at the picture, he is reminded of you. He feels as if you are there. Therefore, he extends the same respect to this picture as he does to you. Similarly, an idol made of metal, paper or clay does not have God in it, but it represents the qualities of God. By looking at the idol, one is reminded of the qualities of God. Metal, paper and clay are only used to make idols or pictures of God. Would anybody speak to the idol and say – 'O Metal, I offer this garland to you? O Paper, I bow to you?' No! Nobody says this. It is because people do not see metal, paper or clay in the idol. They see God in it. They feel the presence of God in the idol. And it is this feeling that bears fruit. Therefore, every devotee worships God using the idol as a medium."

King Mangal Singh got up from his throne and knelt before Swamiji with folded hands. His eyes were filled with tears. For the first time in his life, he had truly understood the real secret behind idol worship. Normally, people perform idol worship, driven by either superstition or ignorance. Similarly, people who oppose idol worship, also do so out of ignorance merely to show off their baseless knowledge. They say that all this is meaningless; what would anyone achieve by worshipping idols made of metal, paper or clay? The fact, however, is that people with both these contrasting beliefs have incomplete knowledge.

King Mangal Singh was also confused with his half-baked knowledge. However, just one encounter with Swamiji had helped in eradicating his ignorance and acquire true knowledge that transcends limiting beliefs.

❑

21
Why do Different Religions and Customs exist?

Blessed are they whose bodies get destroyed in the service of others.

On a pleasant evening, Swami Vivekananda was walking on the roads of Mount Abu, singing Saint Mira's devotional song. Many people were walking along with him while listening to his song. Incidentally, Munshi Faiz Ali was also passing by the same route. He was attracted to the melodious voice of Swamiji and followed him. When the song ended, Swamiji went his way and so did others. However, Munshiji was so engrossed in listening to the song that he did not even notice where Swamiji was headed. As he continued walking further, he reached a cave. When he peered inside, he saw Swami Vivekananda seated inside.

Swamiji smiled, "Who are you looking for? The One you should be looking for, or a servant of His?"

Munshiji was startled by Swamiji's words. He pondered, "What is this monk hinting at? Who should I search for? Is he pointing at the painter of Nature? But until today I have not searched for God. I have only offered Namaz and considered my duty to be done."

Swamiji broke Munshiji from his reverie by inviting him inside. Munshiji entered the cave and asked, "Swamiji, I am highly impressed by your personality, and my curiosity begs you for an answer."

On receiving Swamiji's consent, Munshiji said, "Since childhood, we have been told that Allah is only one. If He is one, He must have created this entire world."

"You said it right," replied Swamiji.

"Then why did God create so many kinds of people? Why did he create so many different religions like Islam, Hinduism, Christianity, Judaism and many others? What was the harm in making everybody alike, so that there would be no differences and fights in the name of religion?"

Swamiji laughed heartily, "How would you find that creation where there is only one type of flowers? How would it be if there were only roses and no lotuses, nor marigolds, nor lilies?"

"Yes! If there were only pulses to eat and we had to eat them every day with the same taste, how boring that world would have been?" said Munshiji, after thinking for a while.

Swamiji explained, "Let's try to understand it with another example. Can you ask a painter to make the same painting every time? No, because the painter is meant for making a variety of paintings. He would like to make different kinds of paintings to express himself completely. He would not be satisfied with just one painting. God is the greatest of all painters. How can His expression be complete by creating just one type of human being? God created pictures of us so that He can express Himself to the fullest of His possibilities and attain its pinnacle. This is why He has created such diverse kinds of organisms and human beings on earth. As far as religion is concerned, it has not been created by God. Man has created a religion for his convenience."

Munshiji expressed another tormenting thought, "But why is it that one religion permits people to eat both beef and pork, whereas another permits only pork, and yet in other, only beef?"

Swami Vivekananda laughed out loud, "Has the Lord issued any such directive?"

"But people say so," replied Munshiji.

Swamiji explained, "The food habits of any region is a product of its local habitat. Can people living on the seashore do farming in the sea? No, naturally their food will have a predominance of aquatic life. On the other hand, people living on fertile land adopt agriculture as their profession. They grow grains and other kinds of food crops. They also rear animals easily. Therefore, people of these regions consider Mother Earth, the life-giving rivers and cows like their mother. All three play an important role in agriculture.

"At the same time, how can one cultivate in a desert? Since food grains cannot be harvested in those regions, those people depend on animals for food. How can a vegetarian survive in the odd climatic conditions of Tibet? So is the case with Arabian countries too. Hindus maintain that one should take a bath before going to the temple or performing worship. Contrary to this, Muslims believe that before offering Namaz, it is sufficient to wash your hands and face with a little water. There is a reason for this practice. The Arabian countries do not have enough water for bathing five times a day before offering Namaz. This is possible only in India where several rivers and springs flow and so are the wells filled with water. In Tibet, though water is available, it is so cold that if a person bathes five times a day, he would be frozen to death. All these customs are not created by God to divide humanity; rather, these rules and regulations are made by man himself for the sake of convenience."

Swamiji continued his conversation by citing yet another context, "When a person dies, the last rites have to be performed on the dead body. In Arabian countries, there has always been a dearth of trees, and sand is in abundance. Hence, the custom of burial has come to be practised there. In a country like India, there are trees in huge numbers; wood is easily available. Due to the huge population, the land is not abundant. Hence the custom of cremation came into being here. So, the customs originated, depending upon the facilities available in a given region."

Munshiji responded, "It means that we should perform the last rites as per the resources available in a given region, and not according to the beliefs and customs of any specific religion."

Swami Vivekananda agreed, "Indeed, it should be like that!"

Munshiji further asked, "Will the Lord be angry if the dead body of a Muslim is cremated or that of a Hindu is buried?"

Swamiji laughed aloud, "The Lord never gets angry with his children. He is the ocean of love and compassion. There is no reason to be afraid of Him. He should only be loved."

"In fact, we are afraid of those, whom we do not love. The fright of the Lord has been used to persuade people to perform noble deeds in society. However, if people are performing good deeds out of fear, then such deeds do not hold any significance. One should not tread the path of righteousness out of fear; rather it should be the result of understanding, love, faith and respect for God. Mostly, people put the Lord in their shoes and think that certain acts of theirs will annoy Him. If God gets annoyed, then what is the difference between Him and a common man? It is sheer ignorance on the part of man to be afraid of God. Praying to God is the outcome of knowledge, and nurturing divine love and becoming one with God is the consequence of true wisdom."

❑

22
King of Khetri and Swami Vivekananda

All knowledge that the world has ever received comes from the mind; the infinite library of the universe is in our mind.

Swami Vivekananda was in search of such noble people, with whose help he could propagate the work of Mother Goddess, as directed by his guru. During his journey, Swamiji came across King Ajit Singh, the king of Khetri. He was the kind of person that Swamiji was looking for.

Within a few days of their acquaintance, the King and Swamiji were so inspired by each other's thoughts that it seemed as if they were friends for years. Sometimes, even the distinction between king and monk did not exist between them. Swamiji had many kingly qualities within him, and Ajit Singh was also discovering the monk in himself. It was as if they were born to help each other and complement each other. Ajit Singh had no intentions of becoming someone unique who stayed in an ivory tower. He was fond of music as well as devotion. Very often he fancied spending the night in the temple singing devotional songs. Besides, he loved writing poetry.

Hunting lions in the forest, skinning them and selling their hides was Ajit Singh's family business. When Swamiji came to know of this business, he explained to the king, "When we get scared of any animal, we become violent with it. If I do not harbour fear for anybody, I would never become violent with anybody. Then, even the lion would also not become ferocious towards me. This is the law of nature. There is only one solution to this – win over the fear and violence that dwells in your mind. I am quite confident that you can do it. Both the Lord, as well as His illusion, is pleased with you."

After receiving such a profound understanding of Swami Vivekananda, the king firmly resolved not to hunt any animal ever again. Swamiji's thoughts influenced Ajit Singh to such an extent that gradually he became his ardent devotee.

Once the royal priest came to meet the king. In fact, he had been informed that King Ajit Singh had brought home a monk from Mount Abu. This news had immensely distressed the priest.

When the king saw his priest perturbed, he asked him the reason. The priest replied, "I saw a monk's robe drying in the topmost chamber of your palace. Your Highness may not be aware of the indication, but the scriptures say that the goddess of wealth does not reside where a monk's robe is set to dry. Such a palace also turns into a monastery within no time. Your Highness! Please pay heed to my suggestion. Kindly put this monk up in some other mansion and deploy ten or twenty servants at his disposal. But please do not get a monk stay in the palace. It is not advisable."

The king gravely replied, "The monk's robe is far more attractive to me than the goddess of wealth. I want to see this palace transformed into a monastery. This palace will become more sattvic if it resonates with the chanting of sacred mantras instead of the jingles of dancing girls. Wouldn't everybody experience peace here if this place is dominated by the austere silence of the monks instead of the outcry for wealth and domestic power?"

The priest gaped in utter disbelief. Such arguments, coming from the king, were least expected. He had assumed that his warnings would have deeply impacted the king and that he would at once make some other alternative lodging arrangement for the monk, but what happened was just the opposite.

The royal priest responded with great modesty, "Your Highness! I beg your pardon. But do you know what you are saying? It is fine that you have no interest in royal luxuries, but all the same, it also does not befit you to have your regal bearing biting the dust."

The king replied aptly, "O venerable priest! You are indeed right. You may easily find the ochre robe, but not the association of a true monk for free. In search of the ultimate Truth, these hermits perform severe austerities in the Himalayas for several years. In this land of Rajputana, there are so many kingdoms and royal families, but have you found a true monk anywhere in this kingdom? Royalty is steeped in sensual enjoyments everywhere. Do you notice even an iota of renunciation?

"O priest, the kingdom is God's illusion that binds us to this world and tests our attachment towards the world. But the association of a monk is the proof of divine grace. It is not rare to become a king, but it is rare to be a true monk."

The royal priest found the king's behaviour quite insulting and inappropriate.

Lowering his tone, the king again asked the priest, "Before me, hasn't anyone become a monk? Why are you so troubled at all? Many times, it is you who have discussed that our existence is not limited to our bodies and that all worldly relations are merely an illusion. The true relationship can be established with God alone. Today, when I am considering your statements to be true, you want to forbid me. Is transcendental knowledge a mere topic for discussion? Should it not be put into practice?"

"When you put that to practice, all worldly bondages break off," the priest replied.

The king replied, "You see what falls off, but have you not seen what is attained! I have found someone who has implemented this wisdom in his life and has achieved what one attains after renouncing the world. Now, are you asking me to consider this knowledge to be true, while also forbidding me from putting it into practice? I can't live this false life of double standards."

This incident reflects King Ajit Singh's devotion to Swami Vivekananda and that he had indeed started implementing the wisdom he was receiving from Swamiji in his own life.

Swami Vivekananda's change of attire

King Ajit Singh was preparing for a pilgrimage to Jin Mata. He had ordered for several dresses for the same. When Swamiji saw those many dresses, he laughed out, "Your Highness! What is this? You have got an entire shop full of dresses for you!"

The king replied, "Swamiji, all these dresses are meant for you. You will have to do horse riding during the pilgrimage. For comfortable horse riding, you will need to wear these dresses. You would not be able to travel in your present attire mainly because of the extreme heat and cold of Rajputana. If you catch a cold, you may fall ill. Therefore, you must tie a turban on your head. In Rajasthan, there are several ways of tying a turban, each state and region has its style. You may adopt any style you like, but you must cover your head. Also, God forbid, but if you were to fall off the horse, the turban would avert any injury."

Swamiji smiled, "In the name of horse riding, you wish to change the attire of a monk!"

Despite Swamiji's consistent protest, King Ajit Singh did not give up. He presented several logical reasons to persuade Swamiji. Ultimately, Swamiji asked, "O king! What do you want?"

With folded hands, the king humbly said, "Please give up your insistence regarding your attire and wear attire that is required for your protection. Swamiji, we ought to sometimes change ourselves as per the needs of the time and place."

Swami Vivekananda had to give in to King Ajit Singh's genuine feeling for him. He was very pleased with the king's devotion. After that, he adopted the turban and ochre robes as a part of his attire.

King Ajit Singh was so impressed by Swamiji that he also wished to become a monk like him and travel along with him. He even discussed this with Swamiji. Though Swamiji was quite delighted to hear the king's thoughts, he very well knew the purpose of the king's life. He explained, "O King! I can understand your devotion, but you are born with a specific purpose. You have a responsible role to play as a patron for significant events that will transform the world. Never relinquish your kingdom and continue to be the king. To execute the responsibility that you are entrusted with, you ought to fulfil the duty of a ruler and perform a lifelong penance."

King Ajit Singh understood the purport of Swamiji's statement and promised him that he would always abide by his guidance.

❑

23

Value of Self-experience, Futility of the Illusory World

Experience is the only teacher we have.

Swami Vivekananda used to be approached by the youth from various cults and sects. They were all influenced by some social reform movement or the other and wanted to bring about a revolution in society. Swamiji could see that they were heading in the wrong direction as they could comprehend only one aspect of reform.

The assistant professor of Chemistry at the Christian College could not put up with the fame of Swami Vivekananda. Being envious of the Swami's popularity, he finally decided to meet Swamiji and challenge him. Since he was a Christian himself, he believed that it was only by being a Christian that one can truly derive the benefit of religion in practical life. He could not see any utility of Hinduism. He came to meet Swamiji with his hidden agenda of trampling upon his honour.

Swami Vivekananda was meditating with his eyes closed. The professor sat in front of him and waited for him to open his eyes. As soon as Swamiji opened his eyes, the professor said, "Look Swamiji, the world has so much pleasure and comforts to offer. There is love, good relations, wealth and prosperity, a variety of attire… farms and fields. You have turned away from all of this and are seeking out for a God who asks you to relinquish all of these. What would you derive by loving such a God?"

Swamiji smiled, "Had you met Lord Buddha earlier; he would have come to know from you that there is so much pleasure in this world! Why then would he have said that the world is full of misery! Had you met Jesus Christ, would he have declared that it is easier for a camel to pass through the eye of a needle than for a rich man to enter the kingdom of God! If you had met Lord Krishna, he would not have propagated the idea of detachment. Indeed, you have arrived on this earth so late!"

The professor became furious, "Are you ridiculing me, Swamiji?"

Swamiji replied, "No, I am only expressing my condolences."

Unable to understand the purport of Swamiji's words, the professor asked, "Then tell me, for what pleasure should one renounce these worldly pleasures? What is there to be achieved, that one should give up the pleasures of his senses?"

Swamiji replied, "Can you make a little child understand that there are more valuable objects available in this world than the earthen horse or other toys he plays with? Can you ask him to cast away his toy horse and get a real one? You speak just like that child, who is unwilling to leave his toy horse."

The professor was stunned to hear Swami Vivekananda's reply.

Now Swamiji elaborated further on the aspect of sensual pleasures, "Man controls his five senses with his mind. However, due to lack of discipline, he wanders around chasing after these sensual pleasures. He thinks that he will be content after satisfying the cravings of his senses. However, in the end, he realises that despite tending to his senses, his craving has not subsided. On the contrary, the pursuit of satisfying his senses has only magnified and multiplied his negative tendencies. Chasing material pleasures is like pouring oil into the fire. The fire of craving can never be quenched. Therefore, instead of gratifying the unending desires of the senses, adopt a middle path. Bring a balance in the usage of your senses.

"Today, in the pursuit of his sensual pleasures, man has started forgetting the values of humanity, ethics, spontaneity, and even the purpose of life itself. Therefore, we need to awaken our conscience about the craving for materialistic desires. Instead of delving into the extremes of any enjoyment and losing ourselves, we should exercise self-control. Very soon, self-restraint will become a part of our nature. With this, our senses will help us in building our character instead of ruining it.

"I love you and wish that you cast away your adamancy and embrace true wisdom. Real happiness doesn't lie in sensual pleasures, but in attaining the ultimate wisdom."

The professor modestly smiled, "How can I continue with my adamancy in front of you, Swamiji? Your simple rationale has shattered my ego. From today, please accept me as your loyal disciple."

Swamiji blessed him, "Professor, you are indeed a very loving and pure-hearted soul. May God bless you!"

Through a simple conversation, Swami Vivekananda had dissolved the Christian professor's ego and bestowed upon him the first ray of wisdom.

❑

24

The Proposal to Participate in the Parliament of Religions

Purity, perseverance and energy – these three I want.

Every incident that happens in one's life, whether it's major or trivial, happens by one's divine plan. The divine plan is a natural way of bringing the highest possibilities in your life. You only need to remain receptive to its natural unfolding. If you do not create obstacles of negative thoughts in its way, you will automatically advance towards your highest potential. Then you would be encouraged to effortlessly move in the direction of physical vitality, mental maturity, financial independence, social harmony and spiritual progress. This can be called as the divine plan.

We ought to be prepared to receive the best things in life by our divine plan. Very often, we tend to hold onto fixed ways of how things should happen in our lives. But it helps to let go and allow things to unfold naturally as per our divine plan, in perhaps a different or a better way.

Pray for the best circumstances in which that thing should appropriately come to you. When you ask for right cues from nature, nature always guides you precisely in the right direction. You come to intuitively know about the next step that you should take in your life. The divine plan manifested in this precise way in the life of Swami Vivekananda.

Hari Babu from Khandwa informed Swamiji about the upcoming Parliament of World's Religions being held in the city of Chicago in America. He suggested that Swami Vivekananda should participate in this conference as an Indian representative. Swamiji had also heard about the Parliament of Religions while he was in Porbandar and Junagarh. Therefore, he told Hari Babu, "I wish I could do that, but I have to go on a pilgrimage to Rameshwaram. If I halt at every place on my way, I would never be able to reach Rameshwaram."

In this way, Swamiji did not approve both the proposals of attending the Parliament of World's Religions, because as per the divine plan, the proposal was to be approved in Madras.

Triplicane Literary Society of Madras had organised Swami Vivekananda's lecture in the city of Madras. About a hundred selected scholars from the city were invited to attend his lecture. Everybody considered Swami Vivekananda to be an unprecedented orator. His impressive personality was an expression of extraordinary intelligence, unfathomable knowledge, unflinching patriotism and signs of a true monastic.

At the event, Mr. Perumal proposed that Swami Vivekananda should be sent to the Parliament of World's Religions in Chicago as a representative of Hindu religion. The entire assembly approved the proposal with a thunderous applause. Swamiji was also startled to witness the enthusiasm of the crowd.

After the event, Swamiji asked Mr. Perumal, "Had you come prepared with this proposal? How can your Literary Society decide my visit to Chicago? Can your organisation bear all the expenses of my visit?"

Mr. Perumal replied, "No. But our next step will be to buy in some of the patronages of some influential people from society into this venture. We will form a committee and raise funds for your journey. We will also collect donations from those who have already agreed to support you."

Mr. Perumal and his friends began collecting funds for Swamiji's journey. Mr. Manmathnath donated five hundred rupees for this noble cause and initiated the effort. Mr. Perumal was very enthusiastic about this work. He even went from door to door with the hope of getting money, be it a poor man's hut or a rich man's mansion. Some gave a paisa; others contributed a rupee or even one hundred rupees as per their capacity. However, he welcomed everyone.

Swami Vivekananda was also excited by his disciples' vigour. The discussion of his visit to America had started since long, but now it was gathering momentum and taking shape. It was indeed the Mother Goddess' wish, a divine plan. Swamiji had not made any efforts from his side. Whenever he was offered some money, he politely disapproved it. Now the Mother Goddess Herself had started organising everything in the guise of his disciples. Swamiji also started preparing himself to attend the Parliament of Religions.

After a few days, Mr. Perumal informed Swamiji about the amount collected. Swami Vivekananda got a jolt after hearing the amount. He wanted an indication from the Mother Goddess whether whatever was happening was as per Her will. He closed his eyes and went into deep meditation.

After a while, Swami Vivekananda opened his eyes and smilingly said, "Take this money and distribute it amongst the poor. I am waiting for the Mother's instruction. I can't proceed in the dark. First and foremost, the Mother has to reveal Her will. If my going to America is Her will, the money would come by itself."

Mr. Perumal was dumbstruck with Swamiji's remarks. He couldn't understand what he should do. He had no other option but to follow his guru's command.

❑

25
Revisit to Khetri

Neither procrastinate nor search but wait for what God sends as per His will. This is my formula.

King Ajit Singh of Khetri was disappointed when he learned about funds being collected to send Swamiji to attend the Parliament of World's Religions in Chicago. He directed his minister to immediately go to Madras and bring Swami Vivekananda along with him with all solemnity.

After reaching Madras, the minister, with much difficulty, got the address of Mr. Manmathnath. When he reached his house, a vehicle came and stopped in front of him. Swami Vivekananda, with two other gentlemen, alighted from the vehicle.

The minister went forward and touched Swamiji's feet. Swamiji was surprised to see the minister there. He asked, "Munshiji! What brings you here? Is everything alright in Khetri?"

The minister replied, "Swamiji, by your grace everything is fine in Khetri. Ever since Prince Jai Singh was born to the royal couple, His Highness is very anxious to meet you. He is unable to celebrate the birth of the newborn prince in the absence of his guru. The birth celebration of the prince is incomplete without your blessings. Therefore, I bring his request to come with me to Khetri."

Taking his seat, Swamiji replied, "King Ajit Singh is a dear friend of mine. I also want to be a part of his happy moments. But

I have decided to go to America at the end of this month. I am busy preparing for my visit. I hope you understand my point, Munshiji."

The minister kept staring at Swamiji and then knelt down before him. He started pleading him to accompany him. Swamiji replied, "I can understand that King Ajit Singh would be very unhappy if I don't accompany you. To hurt him in any manner is a sin for me. But I can't leave all this work incomplete and come along with you."

The minister assured Swami Vivekananda, "The entire responsibility of your foreign travel now lies with King Ajit Singh. He would make all the arrangements. You do not have to worry about that account. Please come to Khetri for once." He further continued, "The king is also displeased by the fact that the expenses of your foreign visit are being organised from some other sources. Being your disciple, it is the king's right to bear that expense. Why is he being deprived of his right?"

Hearing this, Swamiji saw a new ray of hope. It implied that as per the divine plan, the expenses for his foreign visit would be borne by the honest wealth of King Ajit Singh. Now he could understand why the Mother Goddess did not allow him to accept the money from the kings of Mysore and Ramnad, or from the aristocracy of Hyderabad. That money was supposed to come from the treasury of King Ajit Singh.

The moment Swamiji learned that everything was happening as per his divine plan, he said, "Manmath Babu! I would have to leave for Khetri at the earliest." His words reflected his resolve.

Swamiji was accorded a royal reception at Khetri. He saw light extending in all directions. The entire city was decked up for his welcome as if all the citizens were celebrating the festival of Diwali. As soon as Swamiji arrived, King Ajit Singh prostrated before him. Swamiji spent three weeks in Khetri amidst joy and merriment. The time of his departure was approaching. Swami Vivekananda blessed both the Queen and the new-born prince.

In those days, Swami Vivekananda was known as "Vividishanand". Before he left Khetri, King Ajit Singh said, "For a person who is the knower of the Truth, the name 'Vividishanand' is not appropriate. Moreover, it is also difficult to pronounce. The common people cannot understand its meaning. Therefore, in my opinion, you should change your name."

Swamiji smiled, "I am a seeker; I am thirsty for knowledge. Vividisha means inquisitiveness, thirst for knowledge. Now please tell me how I can discard this name? It would change my character representation."

The king replied, "All your disciples believe that your period of Vividisha is now over. You have left it far behind."

"Then in your opinion, what should be my name?" Swamiji enquired smilingly.

The king replied, "In my opinion, you have reached the pinnacle of *Viveka* (the power of discernment of the Truth). Therefore, I would love to address you as 'Swami Vivekananda'. This name is simple and befits your character too. From today, we would like to address you as 'Swami Vivekananda'. Please accept our request."

"O King, as you wish," Swamiji readily accepted the name. However, the king did not stop at that. He took a promise from Swami Vivekananda that henceforth he would introduce himself by this new name and would never change it.

Before that, many people knew Swamiji with different names such as Narendra, Narendra Baba, Nityananda, Sachidananada, Chinmayananda or Vividishananda. However, the new name "Swami Vivekananda", as proposed by King Ajit Singh, became so intensely associated with Narendra that it never changed after that.

❑

26

Blessings of Mother Sarada

Where can we go to find God if we cannot see Him in our hearts and every living being?

For several days, Swami Vivekananda did not have any contact with either his family or the Math. He did not want to have any correspondence on worldly affairs. On the one hand, on the command of the Mother Goddess and his guru, he was preparing himself for his visit to America, and on the other hand, his worldly relations and attachments were pulling him back. However, no thought could hold back his zeal as he had mentally prepared himself for his visit abroad.

Swami Vivekananda had great respect for his mother. When he became the disciple of Ramakrishna Paramhansa, he saw the glimpse of his mother in Thakur's wife, Sarada Devi. He had set out on his journey from Kolkata with the blessings of Mother Sarada. Now, before leaving for Chicago, he went to Mother Sarada to seek her blessings again. However, Mother Sarada sent him back and said, "Come again tomorrow. I would first assess your worthiness and only then give you my blessings."

The next day when Swami Vivekananda arrived, Mother Sarada said, "Well, you have come here to seek my blessings. First hand over that knife to me. I shall give you my blessings after cutting vegetables." Swami Vivekananda was an ardent devotee of Mother Sarada. He at once grabbed the knife and handed it over to her. On receiving the knife, Mother's face lit up. She said, "Go Narendra, my blessings are always with you!"

Swami Vivekananda was utterly astonished. He was expecting Mother Sarada to test him to ascertain his worthiness rigorously, but no such thing happened. Breaking his astonishment, she explained, "Generally, when someone is asked to hand over a knife, he would always hold its handle and direct the pointed end towards the other person. This shows that the person is not bothered by the other person's trouble and convenience. He gives preferencc to his convenience first. However, you did not do so. While giving me the knife, you held its pointed part in your hand and allowed me to hold its handle, so that even by mistake, I don't hurt my finger. This act reflects a monk's mind, who endures all hardships himself and gives happiness to others. This indicates that you are not only eligible to go to Chicago but to all places on earth."

After being blessed by Mother Sarada, Swami Vivekananda danced with ecstasy and shed tears of joy. To control his emotions, he went to the seashore and spent some time sitting there.

In May 1893, some of his disciples bid him their farewell at the harbour, from where he sailed for America.

❑

27
The Divine Plan for Swamiji

Give up jealousy and conceit.
Learn to work unitedly for others.

One who knows that the same Consciousness dwells in every being doesn't feel any separateness from others. For him, the entire universe is bound by the same thread. He would not feel annoyed by the inappropriate behaviour of others. With a steadfast mind, if he helps the other person with the right understanding and expresses gratitude towards him, he will not feel disturbed by the other's inappropriate behaviour. Several incidents from Swami Vivekananda's life reveal his conviction and unwavering mind. Some of these incidents that are explained in this chapter serve as an inspiration to train the mind accordingly.

***

In one such incident, Swamiji and Lallu Bhai were quietly seated together in a train compartment travelling to Boston. While Lallu Bhai was worried about his job, he was also quite concerned about the wellbeing of Swamiji. This was because the kind of behaviour that had been meted out to Swamiji in America could have easily caused anyone to feel despondent.

However, Swamiji did not lose heart, nor did he lose his self-control even for a moment. His mind was so pure and unwavering that none of the incidents could disturb him. Potentially disturbing incidents kept repeating with him one after the other as if Mother Goddess was testing him again and again. However, no incident could pose an obstacle on his path; he continued to move undeterred towards his mission.

A rugged rogue passed by Swamiji very closely. After having a strange look at Swamiji, he started laughing mockingly at him. Another person also looked at Swamiji and gave a wicked smile. However, neither Lallu Bhai nor Swamiji reacted to them. Hence they went away disappointed.

After that, a third person came and tried to snatch his turban. Swamiji tried his best to safeguard his turban with his full might. Laughing unabashedly, the snatcher went away. However, despite such humiliating incidents, Swamiji's mind didn't get distracted at all.

***

The second incident happened with Swamiji when he had been to the Telegraph office in Boston to send a telegram to Mr. Alasinga Perumal in India. He came out of the Telegraph office and started walking quietly. As it was very cold outside, he was rubbing his palms to get some warmth. Suddenly someone pushed him from behind. When he looked back, he found a rogue laughing at him, baring all his teeth. Soon another person arrived at the scene and extending his arm, pinched Swamiji.

Swamiji understood that they were trying to pick up a fight with him. However, Swamiji neither wanted to quarrel nor fight with them. He turned around and started walking swiftly. Both of them stood at the same place and heartily laughed at Swamiji as if they were out to insult Swamiji.

After some time, when Swamiji turned back, he saw a mob of vagabonds and rogues following him. As they could have attacked him anytime, Swamiji ran wherever he found his way. The mob chased him, madly shouting at him. After turning around a couple of bends in the streets, Swamiji hid behind a wall while the crowd went past without noticing him. When the mayhem subsided, Swamiji came out on the street, looked up in the sky and exasperatedly asked, "O God, what kind of test is this?"

***

In the third incident, Swamiji was supposed to visit Dr. John Henry Barrows, the Chairman of the Parliament of World's Religions. Unfortunately, he lost his address. So he decided to scan through the entire city of Chicago by foot and knock on each door to get his address. Swamiji had complete faith in the divine plan of the Almighty. He fully accepted the loss of Dr. Barrow's address and the loss of the little money that he had, as the divine will of God.

Swamiji came out of the Railway yard and asked the first person he met, "Can you please tell me where the office of the Parliament of World's Religions is?" The person was enraged. He said, "You black!" and went away.

Swamiji was perplexed. Then he looked at himself. His ochre robe was fully soiled. His turban was a peculiar form of amusement for the Americans, his complexion was dark, and he had not shaved for the last few days. In such a condition, nobody would regard him as a gentleman. Therefore, he gave up the idea of asking the address of the Parliament from the passerby.

Swamiji opened the gate of the first house he came across. As he was entering, a man came running out of the house. He misbehaved with Swamiji and threw him out of the gate. Swamiji felt inappropriate to stand there any further. Considering it as the wish of the Mother Goddess, he went ahead and stopped in front of another house. There was a charming lady at the door. Before Swamiji could say anything, the lady saw him, screamed and ran inside the house. She was very scared. He decided not to stop there too. He understood that it was not the Mother Goddess' will for him to get any help from there. Swamiji didn't react against the will of the Mother Goddess.

After walking quite a long distance, Swamiji was tired and hungry. He approached a house for alms. The person who opened the door shouted at him and misbehaved with him.

Despite such humiliating behaviour, Swamiji neither felt hatred, nor did he retaliate against anyone. He calmly walked away from that place. He thought, "The land of America also belongs to the Mother Goddess, but it is different from India. Although India is a developing country, under normal circumstances, nobody would die of hunger there. Any common man would certainly give a handful of food grains as alms to a hungry person. Though America is an affluent country, they do not have the custom of giving alms or sympathising with a hungry person or respecting monks. However, a mendicant depends solely on alms. If the Mother Goddess wishes, then I would get alms. If She doesn't, then there would be no alms." He resigned at the feet of the Almighty.

Lost in his thoughts, Swamiji was moving on his way. He had altogether dropped the idea of knocking on the doors and asking for help. He resolved that now he would eat what the Mother would send and go where the Mother would take him. He would depend on the Mother. Swamiji did not know where he was going. He stopped at a place as it was difficult for him to move further without taking rest. He sat on a stone slab by the side of the road.

After some time, a lady came out of the house opposite the slab where he was seated. She was the owner of that house. She approached Swamiji and asked, "Are you a representative of the Parliament of World's Religions?" Swamiji felt as if he had a glimpse of the Mother Goddess in that lady. He explained his entire ordeal to her. She was Mrs. George W. Hale. She belonged to a reputed family of Chicago. She invited Swamiji to her house, served him food and arranged for his rest. After he had rested, she took him to the office of the Parliament of World's Religions and arranged his meeting with Dr. Barrows.

After that meeting, Swamiji was accepted as the official representative of the Hindu religion without any letter of introduction. Mr. & Mrs. John B. Lyons hosted Swamiji at their residence. Both the Hale family and the Lyons couple became lifelong friends of Swami Vivekananda. Swamiji was convinced that the Mother Goddess was always guiding him, even through these helpful people.

These incidents reflect Swamiji's patience, steadfastness of mind and unflinching faith in God. Today's youth should learn from these incidents and inculcate these qualities. The life of Swami Vivekananda is a source of inspiration in itself. Owing to these qualities, he could accomplish his mission in the most adverse circumstances of his life.

❑

28
Dissemination of Wisdom in America

Ask nothing; want nothing in return. Give what you have to give; it will come back to you, but do not think of that now.

In the Parliament of Religions in Chicago, Swamiji started his speech with, "Brothers and Sisters of America." The audience was so delighted to hear this address that their reverberating applause continued for a long time. His speech mesmerised the entire congregation. After that success, Swamiji became an instant fame all over America. Within no time, thousands of people became his disciples.

Through his lecture, Swami Vivekananda glorified both the Hindu religion and India as a nation. He asserted that the Hindu religion is the mother of religions and has taught the world both tolerance and universal acceptance. Explaining how Hinduism believes in universal toleration and accepts all religions as true, he stressed upon the fact that religious unity is not going to come by the triumph of any one of the religions and the destruction of the others. For that, the Christian is not to become a Hindu or a Buddhist, nor a Hindu or a Buddhist to become a Christian. But each must assimilate the spirit of the others and yet preserve his individuality and grow according to his law of growth. He also stated that India had sheltered the persecuted and the refugees of all religions and all nations. With this commendable work, Swami

Vivekananda unfurled the flag of Indian culture in the western world.

Swami Vivekananda used to deliver around twelve to fourteen lectures in a week in America. Many times, he wondered what topic he would speak as by then he had spoken on so many topics. However, he used to get awestruck when he used to listen to himself speaking in front of the audience because he didn't know what he would speak on. He used to start speaking, and the speech would ceaselessly flow spontaneously.

One day, he recalled what his guru Ramakrishna Paramhansa had said. Before his death, Ramakrishna Paramhansa could not eat or speak due to cancer in his throat. Pointing to his disciples, he would say, "So what if I am unable to eat with this throat, from here on I will eat through your throats. I have so many throats here through which I can eat." Swami Vivekananda realised that it was his guru Ramakrishna Paramhansa who was speaking through him. Now he was completely relaxed and assured and free from questions like, "How will I speak? On what topic shall I speak?"

Few days before he would deliver the discourse, he used to realise that he was being guided from within about the details of the topic on which he would speak. He used to note down those points for speaking. This continued even in India.

In his lectures, Swami Vivekananda used to say, "By looking at me, do not form any opinion about my guru because I'm merely an inferior instrument, trying to put across his teachings to the masses." He could say so because he had intellectually observed this during the divine plays he had experienced. Moreover, he experientially realised it. Hence the same experience reflected in his speech as well.

One day, he was very disappointed by mulling over whatever he was doing, pondering what it would lead to. Hearing his lectures, people felt happy due to temporary excitement, but they would soon return to square one. There was hardly any change in anybody. Then, he worked on some selected few people, initiated them and institutionalised such places, where they could work towards the ultimate Truth with zeal and perseverance.

Swami Vivekananda stayed abroad for four years. During this time, he travelled between Chicago, Boston, New York and London. During this period, he had also called over some of his fellow disciples of Ramakrishna Paramhansa to America to support his work. After that, he returned to India. The news of Swamiji's homecoming after his stupendous success at the Parliament of World's Religions infused the minds of common people with limitless energy. The spiritual ambassador of the ancient motherland was returning after fulfilling his mission. They were to accord a suitable welcome to their spiritual leader. Several committees were formed in big cities for this purpose. Swamiji's brother disciples and friends impatiently waited to see him.

After his visit to Colombo, a grand reception was arranged for Swamiji in an open ground in Madras. In another meeting on an open ground in Madras, Swamiji urged the masses to maintain their enthusiasm and extend him all possible help for doing great work in India.

As news about Swamiji was regularly published in the newspapers in India, his countrymen were also aware of him. Wherever he went, people gathered around him and welcomed him warmly. When someone asked him, "Do you feel it is justified to spend so much money for your reception? Do you want such a huge rally to be organised?" Swami Vivekananda replied, "Why not? It is indeed needed. Otherwise, how would people come to know about Ramakrishna Paramhansa? It is His work. His teachings are reaching the masses." From this, it can be seen how the extraordinary disciple was propagating the teachings of his guru.

Further, in the subsequent lectures delivered at Kolkata, Swami Vivekananda said with all honesty, "Whatever, I'm going to preach you now, the statements which will give you wisdom are the master words spoken by my guru Ramakrishna Paramhansa. If any of these statements delude you, rest assured that they are mine!" It shows how Swami Vivekananda used to speak his mind openly, without any deceit. While disseminating the guru's teachings, such words are used so that the ego does not creep in. An honest and deceit-free disciple is different from the rest. When someone praised Swami Vivekananda and asked him about his guru, he replied, "Collectively, thousands of disciples like me cannot equate even a millionth part of my guru."

It was Swamiji's constant realisation that Ramakrishna Paramhansa was always backing him, enlivening all his actions. He would say, "Ramakrishna Paramhansa is far greater than the disciples can even fathom. He is the source of infinite spiritual ideas that can be developed in infinite ways. One glance of his gracious eyes can create a hundred thousand Vivekananda at this instant. If he now chooses to work through me as His instrument, I can only bow to His will."

After returning to India in 1899, Swami Vivekananda established the Belur Math, the present headquarters of the Ramakrishna Math. He constituted a board of trustees with the monks in order and handed over the responsibility of managing the affairs of the Math to them. The main objective of the Math was to train the monks in spiritual practice and to serve humanity in all possible ways. With the establishment of the Belur Math, the independent existence of Ramakrishna Math came to an end.

After that, a separate organisation named Ramakrishna Mission was founded and registered in the year 1909. Its management was handed over to a governing body consisting of the Trustees of the Belur Math. Both the Ramakrishna Math and Ramakrishna Mission now have branches all over India.

The objective of Ramakrishna Mission is to propagate all those principles which Ramakrishna Paramhansa imparted and expressed during his lifetime for the welfare of humanity, to help humanity to use these principles for their physical, mental and spiritual well-being.

Swami Vivekananda was extremely delighted to see the expansion and propagation of the work done by Ramakrishna Mission and Ramakrishna Math in various areas.

❑

29
Final Days

Hold on to faith and strength; be true, be honest, be pure, and don't quarrel amongst yourselves. Jealousy is the bane of our race.

During his final days, Swamiji tried to spend a peaceful life in the Math.

Day by day, his physical health was deteriorating, but his mind was still alert. There were no signs of improvement in his health. However, it did not affect his work. When one of his disciples requested him to take some rest, he replied, "Brother! Where is the time to take rest? The 'Kali' whom Ramakrishna Paramhansa used to call out had entered this body a couple of days before his death. It is She who is leading me here and there to various places for his work. She does not allow me to remain stable at a place to look after my mortal well-being."

Swamiji had some pet birds and animals inside the Math, including a dog, a tiger, a goat, a swan, a deer, a stork, some cows, sheep, and ducks. He relaxed with them. All the animals and birds were fond of him. Swamiji was an ocean of love, so these birds and animals were also not deprived of his love either.

For a long time, Swamiji was under the supervision of his physicians. His condition was deteriorating. Both his legs were swollen, and his body had become extremely sensitive. He had almost no sleep at all. On the advice of one of the doctors, he had entirely given up the intake of water and salt. He did not take even a single drop of water for twenty-one days. During this time, he told one of his disciples, "The body is, after all, an equipment of our mind. Whatever the mind commands, the body has to obey. Now I do not even think about water, and its absence does not bother me. It feels as if I can do anything."

Considering his poor health, his fellow disciples tried to place restrictions on his activities and regulate his conversation with spiritual seekers; but Swamiji did not approve of that. One day, he said, "Look! What is the utility of this body? It should always be in the service of people. Didn't Thakur preach until the last moment of his life? I should also follow his footsteps. I do not care if this body perishes. You can't imagine how much joy I derive by getting a chance to speak to genuine spiritual seekers. I am ready to die time and again to awaken the souls of my friends."

Seeing how Swamiji's life was becoming centred in meditation, his disciples and fellow men became worried. They recalled the words of Ramakrishna Paramhansa, "After completing his mission, Narendra would immerse himself in Samadhi forever. When he realises his true nature, he will refuse to live in his mortal body." Undaunted, Swami Vivekananda saw the impending death of his body.

During the last few days, he had given up his responsibilities almost completely. He had a feeling that he would not be able to complete his fortieth year of life. Now, the responsibility of the Math lay on the other disciples of Ramakrishna Paramhansa.

Swamiji's health was deteriorating rapidly, and it was a matter of concern for his fellow disciples and followers. Bengal's climate was not suitable for him, and it worsened his asthma all the more. Considering his poor health condition, he was advised to take complete rest. To appease his well-wishers, he rested in Belur Math for seven months.

Swami Vivekananda liked his room in the Math. He did his writing and practised meditation in that room. Sometimes, he even took his meals in the same room. Finally, he entered into the state of Maha-Samadhi in the same room and left for his heavenly abode.

❑

30
The Teachings of Swami Vivekananda

Bless people when they revile you. Think how much good they are doing by helping to stamp out the false ego.

Swami Vivekananda has been a source of inspiration for the young generation and will always remain so. He would always be considered as the epitome of knowledge, inspiration, and karma.

During his tour of America, he was once taking a stroll on the banks of a river. He noticed some boys standing on a bridge on the river with an air gun. As he approached them, he saw them trying to shoot at some egg shells floating on the river. However, none of them could hit the target correctly despite multiple attempts. Swamiji patiently watched their practice with keen interest. Then he went over to them and asked for the gun from one of the boys. He aimed at a floating eggshell and hit it in his first shot itself. The boys were surprised to see that he hit the mark in the very first attempt. After that, he fired the gun twelve times and hit an eggshell every time. Every shot was precise and accurate. The boys were awestruck on seeing his skill. They could not contain themselves and asked him, "How could you do it? How could you aim all the shots correctly?"

Swami Vivekananda replied, "Well, the secret is a complete focus on the goal. Whatever you do, do it with absolute concentration. Put your heart and soul into it. When you were shooting, your mind should have focused only on the target. That way, you would never miss your target. When you will focus single-pointedly on the job at hand, then alone can you attain success in your life."

Those were the golden words of Swami Vivekananda with a very deep meaning. If one understands this completely, then even the impediments on his way to the goal would turn out to be stepping stones. All those, who have reached the pinnacle of success in their lives, have functioned with peak focus and concentration. That is why they are known for their extraordinary accomplishments even today. They first set their goal of life and then proceeded towards it with full unwavering focus. They also fulfilled their worldly obligations and kept moving towards the goal.

Swami Vivekananda gave many such valuable teachings to the youth. He taught the youth of India to tread on the path of the highest order and also how to serve others without any expectations. It was Swamiji's dream to see India emerge as a fearless and strong nation. Hence, he gave a powerful message on "Weakness and cowardice are sins, and everybody should be free from them."

Various incidents of Swami Vivekananda's life give a glimpse of how his life was progressing. Several profound messages emerged out of his teachings. Many foreigners were also influenced by his teachings and became his disciples. When somebody asked him why India had not ever conquered any country, Swamiji replied, "It is because Indians take pride in not wanting to conquer any country." He used to say with great conviction that the Sun would rise from the East; meaning the Sun of knowledge will rise from the East. His disciples used to gather and discuss various topics with him. Those who wanted to work sincerely were initiated.

Above all, Swamiji stressed that man's body should be as strong as steel, and his brain should not be dull. It implies that he must possess a strong physique and a sharp brain. People, often out of ignorance, collect and harbour the garbage of negative thoughts in their minds. Those who get involved in matters of weakness, get easily trapped in illusion.

Swamiji used to emphasise the importance of exercises. He always said, "If your body is healthy, it supports you to perform spiritual practice easily." He often said, "If you want to realise God and remember Him, then you must remember Him in the same manner as a widow remembers her husband. If you remember God with the same intensity, you will surely realise Him."

Throughout his life, Swami Vivekananda followed the teachings of his guru to the core. He practised whatever he preached. Another important teaching was, "It is better to wear out the body in doing something selfless rather than to live a thousand years lethargically doing nothing." He worked incessantly until his last moment, visited several places. Work was worship for him. He continued to work even when his body became weak and diseased. In the year 1902, at the age of thirty-nine years, he gave up his mortal body.

Through his teachings, he advised how to make the best use of the body. What kind of life are we leading? What kind of life are people leading as householders? A self-centred householder is least interested in doing anything for others; they merely lead a selfish life and die as if they never really lived. He wanted that people should work with an open heart. He also talked about giving alms, and which alms are superior to the rest. The most superior alms is the giving of spiritual wisdom, then comes the alms of knowledge, followed by alms of life energy, followed by alms of food.

He further said, "You all have already given enough 'alms of food'. In India, even a beggar shares his food with his neighbour.

You have learnt a lot about alms of food. Now you must learn about 'spiritual alms' which would help you in your development. It, however, does not mean that you stop the 'alms of food', rather you need to continue doing so, as you have mastered that. You ought to surpass whatever you have already learnt; now is the time for you to give 'spiritual alms'."

One of his main teachings was that everybody should practice "give and take" policy and remain content with whatever is obtained by that practice. He believed that India should impart spiritual knowledge to the world and in return, accept whatever she gets peacefully. Swami Vivekananda accepted whatever help he received from the West, and we can see its outcome.

The life of Swami Vivekananda has been presented to you. Ramakrishna Paramhansa was the main guiding force of his life. Swamiji could comprehend the divine play of his guru much later. Though Ramakrishna Paramhansa knew the answers to Narendra's questions, he externally behaved like an ignorant person. It was all a part of his divine play. Initially, Swami Vivekananda could not understand his play so he could not derive joy during those years. Later, he realised it through his own experience.

It was only on account of his master's divine play and grace that Swami Vivekananda could communicate and help the Western world understand these aspects of life, which would otherwise have been difficult for them. He could convey the message of awakening internal strength and could explain how one can always keep his ideas before him and attain great heights.

❑

31
An Exemplary Combination of Karma and Truth-Discernment

Combine seriousness with childlike naïveté.
Live in harmony with all. Give up all idea of egoism, and entertain no sectarian views. Useless wrangling is a great sin.

Swami Vivekananda had the power of unselfishness due to which he had a grand outlook encompassing the welfare of all. He was aware that India's situation was weak and deeply felt that something had to be done for its citizens – hungry people should get food... needy people's requirements should be fulfilled... everyone should have access to spiritual knowledge. When he visited the West, he was particularly impressed by their work efficiency, productivity and industrialisation.

He said, "There has to be an exchange between India and the West. India can give them spiritual knowledge and they, in turn, can give industry and work efficiencies to India. Indians are introvert, so they have a wealth of spirituality, while westerners are extrovert. Hence they have immensely worked on material progress and made significant discoveries. If these two join hands, a great power of balance can be created."

What Swami Vivekananda dreamed of could have brought about a state of balance in the world, where every country would have become prosperous scientifically, industrially and spiritually. Now let us consider how this balance can be achieved in our lives.

The power of discerning the Truth first touches at the mental level by gaining knowledge. One gathers information about the world. Then it touches the level of the intellect whereby one conducts experiments in the world's laboratory and tests this knowledge to build one's understanding of the Truth. Then it touches deeper at the level of true Being; wherein one abides by the experience of Consciousness and experiences bliss, which transcends the dualities of sorrow and joy. The life of Swami Vivekananda also passed through these stages and after that, he became Vivekananda (the bliss arising from the power of discernment of Truth).

Now examine for yourself, of all these levels, where does your power of discernment stand today? Have you attained the power of discernment at the mental level, or further at the intellectual level, or ultimately at the bliss level? Wherever we are, we need to move a step higher.

The need of the hour is that every person should achieve knowledge at the mental level, test it in the laboratory of the world at the intellectual level, and ultimately attain transcendental bliss by realising one's true nature. It is very important that we develop the power of discernment at each of these levels. Only then can we attain fulfilment in all areas of life. Then we wouldn't face scarcity of worldly wealth, nor that of spiritual wealth. Now let us understand this balance more deeply.

The number "8" can be symbolically used to understand this all-important balance to be achieved in life. The central part of the digit "8" represents the point of balance. It is by dwelling at the centre that we can establish balance in our lives.

The number "8" has two rounded parts at the top and bottom. The lower round represents Consciousness while the upper round represents expression in the external world. The meeting point between the two round parts is the balancing point from where it is easy to access both.

One round part represents your expression in the external world, consisting of worldly affairs such as relationships, occupation, etc. The other round part represents the spiritual side, dwelling on the experience of Consciousness.

If you remain embroiled only with mundane material affairs, the worldly side of the "8" will grow bigger, and the spiritual side will become smaller. If you attain the ultimate Truth, but not express it in the world, the spiritual part will grow bigger, but that of worldly expression will become smaller. This will also disturb the balance because you would be deprived of the joy of creation. The balancing point not only connects with the experience of the Self but also with success in the external world.

It is only when we establish a balance between the spiritual side and the worldly side that we can bring true harmony in life. If either of these round parts is neglected or over-emphasised, it becomes smaller or bigger and can disturb the much-needed balance in life, leading to lack of fulfilment. To strike this balance, you have to learn the fine art of residing at the centre of the "8". You need to meditate on this centre, so that transition between both these facets of life becomes easier.

After understanding the life of Swami Vivekananda, embark on the journey of raising your power of discernment. May your journey be successful!

❑

A graphical representation of the balance between worldly life and spiritual life

Expression in the world (Neglected)	Expression in the world (Over-emphasized)	Worldly focus (Balanced but limited)
Spiritual Attunement (Over-emphasized)	Spiritual attunement (Neglected)	Consciousness (Balanced but limited)

Balanced and fully evolved life

Power of Truth-discernment in the world

Abiding in Consciousness

Appendix

Swami Vivekananda – Reflections

1. Be free; hope for nothing from anyone. I am sure if you look back on your lives you will find that you were always vainly trying to get help from others which never came.
2. As different streams having different sources all mingle their waters in the sea, so different tendencies, various though they appear, crooked or straight, all lead to the God.
3. Condemn none; if you can stretch out a helping hand, do so. If you cannot, fold your hands, bless your brothers and let them go their way.
4. Never think there is anything impossible for the soul. It is the greatest heresy to think so. If there is a sin, this is the only sin to say that you are weak, or others are weak.
5. If money helps a man to do good to others, it is of some value; but if not, it is simply a mass of evil, and the sooner it is got rid of, the better.
6. If faith in ourselves had been more extensively taught and practised, I am sure a very large portion of the evils and miseries that we have would have vanished.
7. We must encourage everyone in his struggle to live up to his own highest ideal and strive at the same time to make the ideal as near as possible to the Truth.
8. When an idea exclusively occupies the mind, it is transformed into an actual physical or mental state.

9. You have to grow from the inside out. None can teach you; none can make you spiritual. There is no other teacher but your soul.
10. Great work requires great and persistent effort for a long time. ...Character has to be established through a thousand stumbles.
11. Have you got the will to surmount mountain-high obstructions? If the whole world stands against you sword in hand, would you still dare to do what you think is right?
12. Whatever you think, that you will be. If you think yourselves weak, weak you will be; if you think yourselves strong, strong you will be.
13. Hold to the idea, "I am not the mind, I see that I am thinking, I am watching my mind act," and each day the identification of yourself with thoughts and feelings will grow less, until at last, you can entirely separate yourself from the mind and actually know it to be apart from yourself.
14. I fervently wish no misery ever came near anyone, yet it is that alone that gives us an insight into the depths of our lives, does it not? In our moments of anguish, gates barred forever seem to open and let in many a flood of light.
15. Fill the brain with high thoughts, highest ideals, place them day and night before you, and out of that will come great work.
16. Don't look back—forward, infinite energy, infinite enthusiasm, infinite daring, and infinite patience—then alone can great deeds be accomplished.
17. Are great things ever done smoothly? Time, patience, and indomitable will must show.
18. A few heart-whole, sincere, and energetic men and women can do more in a year than a mob in a century.

19. The remedy for weakness is not brooding over weakness, but thinking of strength.
20. Fear is death; fear is a sin, fear is hell, fear is unrighteousness, fear is wrong life. All the negative thoughts and ideas that are in the world have proceeded from this evil spirit of fear.
21. Death is better than a vegetating ignorant life; it is better to die on the battlefield than to live a life of defeat.
22. The old religions said that he was an atheist who did not believe in God. The new religion says that he is an atheist who does not believe in himself.
23. Have faith in yourselves, and stand upon that faith and be strong; that is what we need.
24. The moment I have realised God is sitting in the temple of every human body, the moment I stand in reverence before every human being and see God in him that moment I am free from bondage, everything that binds vanishes, and I am free.
25. All love is an expansion; all selfishness is a contraction. Love is, therefore, the only law of life. He who loves lives; he who is selfish, is dying. Therefore, love for love's sake, because it is the law of life, just as you breathe to live.
26. Do one thing at a time, and while doing it put your whole Soul into it to the exclusion of all else.
27. Neither seek nor avoid; take what comes. It is liberty to be affected by nothing. Do not merely endure; be unattached.
28. All the powers in the universe are already ours. It is we who have put our hands before our eyes and cry that it is dark.
29. All differences in this world are of degree, and not of kind because oneness is the secret of everything.
30. Blows are what awaken us and help to break the dream. They show us the insufficiency of this world and make us long to escape, to have freedom.

31. Do one thing at a time, and while doing it put your whole soul into it to the exclusion of all else.
32. We are responsible for what we are, and whatever we wish ourselves to be, we have the power to make ourselves. If what we are now has been the result of our own past actions, it certainly follows that whatever we wish to be in the future can be produced by our present actions; so we have to know how to act.
33. Learn everything that is good from others, but bring it in, and in your own way absorb it; do not become others.
34. Feel nothing, know nothing, do nothing, have nothing, give up all to God, and say utterly, "Thy will be done." We only dream this bondage. Wake up and let it go.
35. Take courage and work on. Patience and steady work — this is the only way. Go on; remember — patience and purity and courage and steady work. . . . So long as you are pure, and true to your principles, you will never fail.
36. Comfort is no test of truth. Truth is often far from being comfortable.
37. Each work has to pass through these stages—ridicule, opposition, and then acceptance. Those who think ahead of their time are sure to be misunderstood.
38. The great secret of true success, of true happiness, is this: the man or woman who asks for no return, the perfectly unselfish person, is the most successful.
39. Take up one idea. Make that one idea your life; dream of it; think of it; live on that idea. Let the brain, the body, muscles, nerves, every part of your body be full of that idea, and just leave every other idea alone. This is the way to success, and this is the way great spiritual giants are produced.

40. In a day when you don't come across any problems — you can be sure that you are travelling in the wrong path.
41. Do not wait for anybody or anything. Do whatever you can. Build your hope on none.

❑❑❑

■■■

You can send your opinion or feedback on this book to :

Tej Gyan Foundation, Pimpri Colony, P. O. Box 25,
Pimpri, Pune – 411017 (Maharashtra), INDIA
email : mail@tejgyan.com

Write for Us

We welcome writers, translators and editors to join our team. If you would like to volunteer, please email us at: englishbooks@tejgyan.org or call : +91 90110 10963 or +91 90110 13207

About Sirshree

(Symbol of Acceptance)

Sirshree's spiritual quest which began during his childhood, led him on a journey through various schools of thought and meditation practices. His overpowering desire to attain the truth made him relinquish his teaching job. After a long period of contemplation, his spiritual quest culminated in the attainment of the ultimate truth. Sirshree says, **"All paths that lead to the truth begin differently, but end in the same way—with understanding. Understanding is the whole thing. Listening to this understanding is enough to attain the truth."**

Sirshree is the author of several spiritual books. His books have been translated in more than10 languages and published by leading publishers such as Penguin and Hay House. He is the founder of Tej Gyan Foundation, a not-for-profit organization committed to raising mass consciousness by spreading "Happy Thoughts" with branches in the United States, India, Europe and Asia-Pacific. Sirshree's retreats have transformed the lives of thousands and his teachings have inspired various social initiatives for raising global consciousness.

His works include more than 100 books and 3000 discourses. Various luminaries and celebrities such as His Holiness the Dalai Lama, publishers Mr. Reid Tracy and Ms. Tami Simon and yoga master Dr. B. K. S Iyengar have released Sirshree's books and lauded his work. 'The Source' book series, authored by Sirshree, has sold more than 10 million copies in 5 years. His book *The Warrior's Mirror*, published by Penguin, was featured in the Limca Book of Records for being released on the same day in 11 languages.

Tejgyan... The Road Ahead

What is Tejgyan?

Tejgyan is the existential wisdom of the ultimate truth, which is beyond duality. In today's world, there are people who feel disharmony and are desperately trying to achieve balance in an unpredictable life. Tejgyan helps them in harmonizing with their true nature, the Self, thereby restoring balance in all aspects of their life.

And then there are those who are successful but feel a sense of emptiness or void within. Tejgyan provides them fulfillment and helps them to embark on a journey towards self-realization. There are others who feel lost and are seeking the meaning of life. Tejgyan helps them to realize the true purpose of human life.

All this is possible with Tejgyan due to a very simple reason. The experience of the ultimate truth is always available. The direct experience of this truth is possible provided the right method is known. Tejgyan is that method, that understanding. At Tej Gyan Foundation, Sirshree imparts this understanding through a System for Wisdom – a series of retreats that guides participants step by step

Magic of Ultimate Awakening Retreat

Magic of Ultimate Awakening is the flagship self-realization retreat offered by Tej Gyan Foundation The retreat is conducted in two languages – Hindi and English. The teachings of the retreat are non-denominational (secular).

This residential retreat is held for 3-5 days at the foundation's MaNaN Ashram amidst the glory of mountains and the pristine beauty of nature. This ashram is located at the outskirts of the city of Pune in India, and is well connected by air, road and rail. The retreat is also held at other centres of Tej Gyan Foundation across the world.

Participate in the *Magic of Ultimate Awakening* retreat to attain ageless wisdom through a unique simple 'System for Wisdom' so that you can:

1. Live from pure and still presence allowing the natural qualities of consciousness, viz. peace, love, joy, compassion, abundance and creativity to manifest.
2. Acquire simple tools to use in everyday life which help quieten the chattering mind, revealing your true nature.
3. Get practical techniques to access pure presence at will and connect to the source of all answers (the inner guru).
4. Discover missing links in practices of meditation *(dhyana)*, action *(karma)*, wisdom *(gyana)* and devotion *(bhakti)*.
5. Understand the nature of your body-mind mechanism to attain freedom from tendencies and patterns.
6. Learn practical methods to shift from mind-centred living to consciousness-centred living.

For retreats contact +919921008060 or email: mail@tejgyan.com

A Mini retreat is also conducted, especially for teens (14-17 years) during summer and winter vacations

MaNaN Ashram

Survey No. 43, Sanas Nagar, Nandoshi gaon,Kirkatwadi Phata, Sinhagad Road, Dist. Pune 411024, Maharashtra, India.

About Tej Gyan Foundation

Tej Gyan Foundation (TGF) was established with the mission of creating a highly evolved society through all-round self development of every individual that transforms all the facets of his/her life. It is a non-profit organization founded on the teachings of Sirshree. The foundation has received the ISO certification (ISO 9001:2015) for its system of imparting wisdom. It has centres all across India as well as in other countries. The motto of Tej Gyan Foundation is 'Happy Thoughts'.

TGF is creating a highly evolved society through:

- Tejgyan Programs (Retreats, Courses, Television and Radio Programs, Podcasts)
- Tejgyan Products (Books, Tapes, Audio/Video CDs)
- Tejgyan Projects (Value Education, Women Empowerment, Peace Initiatives)

TGF undertakes projects to elevate the level of consciousness among students, youth, women, senior citizens, teachers, doctors, leaders, organizations, police force, prisoners, etc.

Books can be delivered at your doorstep by registered post or courier. You can request for the same through postal money order or pay by VPP. Please send the money order to either of the following two addresses:

WOW Publishings Pvt. Ltd.

1. Registered Office: E-4, Vaibhav Nagar, Near Tapovan Mandir, Pimpri, Pune 411017.
2. Post Box No. 36, Pimpri Colony Post Office, Pimpri, Pune 411017

Phone No. : 9011013210 / 9623457873

You can also order your copy at the online store:
www.gethappythoughts.org

*Free Shipping plus 10% Discount on purchases above Rs. 300/.

For further details contact:

Tejgyan Global Foundation

Registered Office:
Happy Thoughts Building, Vikrant Complex, Near
Tapovan Mandir, Pimpri, Pune 411017, Maharashtra, India.
Contact No: 020-27411240, 27412576
Email: mail@tejgyan.com

MaNaN Ashram:
Survey No. 43, Sanas Nagar, Nandoshi gaon, Kirkatwadi Phata,
Sinhagad Road, Tal. Haveli, Dist. Pune 411024, Maharashtra, India.
Contact No: 992100 8060.
Hyderabad: 9885558100, **Bangalore:** 9880412588,
Delhi: 9891059875, **Nashik:** 9326967980, **Mumbai:** 9373440985

For accessing our unique 'System for Wisdom' from self-help to self-realization, please follow us on:

happy thoughts...	Website	www.tejgyan.org
YouTube	Video Channel	www.youtube.com/tejgyan For Q&A videos: http://goo.gl/YA81DQ
facebook	Social networking	www.facebook.com/tejgyan
twitter	Social networking	www.twitter.com/sirshree
	Internet Radio	http://www.tejgyan.org/internetradio.aspx

Online Shopping
www.gethappythoughts.org

Pray for World Peace along with thousands of others at 09:09 a.m. and p.m. every day